The bloodiest book ever written!

Inside these pages humans and vampires meet in a culinary Danse Macabre.

Discover blood-curdling recipes from around the world .

You will never be the same!

The Dracula Cookbook of Blood

By Ardin C. Price and Trishna Leszczyc

Original/ First Edition

Mugwort Soup Publications, Huntsville, Alabama

The Dracula Cookbook of Blood

By Ardin C. Price & Trishna Leszczyc

Published by:

Mugwort Soup Publications
Post Office Box 11183
Huntsville, Alabama 35814-1183 U.S.A.

All rights reserved. No part of this book may be reproduced or transmitted in any form or by any means, electronic or mechanical, including photocopying, recording or by any information storage and retrieval system without written permission from the authors, except for the inclusion of brief quotations in a review.

Copyright @ 1993 by Ardin C. Price and Trishna Leszczyc
10 9 8 7 6 5 4 3 2 1
Printing in the United States of America

Library of Congress Cataloging in Publication Data
Price, Ardin C. and Leszczyc, Trishna
The Dracula Cookbook of Blood / by Ardin C. Price and Trishna Leszczyc - 1st. ed., completely rev.
  p.cm.
Bibliography; P.
Includes Index.

ISBN: 1-883281-42-3 $14.95 Softcover

Dedication

To my grandmother, Elizabeth Tataczek, who believed - TL
To my companion, Erik Solomon, who believes - AP
and
To all those who have partaken of blood or wish to,
both living and undead.

Table of Contents

Preface

Chapter One..11

Chapter Two..15

Breakfast and Brunch: Start your night out right.

Chapter Three..25

Midnight Delight: Those between meal snacks..

Chapter Four...45

Soups and Stews: Please porridge NOT!

Chapter Five..65

Main Dishes: Abandon hope all who Entree here.

Chapter Six..83

Puddings: Pudding on the Grits.

Chapter Seven...93

Sausages and more sausages: Links to the past.

Appendix

A- Recipe variations: Puddings and more sausages..115
A+ Herbs and Such...120
B- Direct from the Carpathian Mountains....123
B+ Bat God of the Valley of Oaxaca...................127
O Planning a complete meal............................131

Bibliography
    Vampire Lore..133
    Cookbooks...136
Index...139

Special order forms

PREFACE

The inspiration for a book may come from many sources. This book evolved from late night conversations mingled with pizza and a prediliction for vampire films. *Have you ever tasted blood?* And the ball was rolling.

One trip to a library convinced us that there was enough blood eating going on out there to write a book about it. So we wrote the book.

Read and enjoy! And, yes, we have tried some of the recipes ourselves.

         Ardin C. Price
         Trishna Leszczyc

February, 1993, Los Angeles

Acknowledgments

Robert Eighteen-Bisang, without whom this book never would have been. His practical help was invaluable and his vampire expertise, indispensable.

Aiden Kelly, for his encouragement to write

Kathy McGonnell, the best Transylvanian traveling companion any vampire hunter could wish for.

Linda Walters, whose ability to come up with contingency plans is beyond scope, as is her love and encouragement.

My parents, Josephine and Alfred Falen and my sister, Rebecca Falen, for being Polish.

My grandmother Esther Burke, of whom I have seen too little.

Forrest J Ackerman, John C. Clarkson, Michael Gerard, Ronn Jones, Julie Kelly, Rozanne Meredith, Tony Ramon, Diana-Lynn and Alex Roston, Blair Slavin, Matt Stan, Vicky and Brad Walters.

Also to Miriamne and all the gang at C.A.W., and to the many friends and acquaintances, both living and undead, who wished to remain nameless. Whose encouragements are greatly appreciated.

Warning-Disclaimers

Cooking with blood is a serious pastime and proper precautions must be maintained. As with all cooking proper temperatures and storage are of concern.

If you taste a mixture before it is cooked just put a bit to your mouth and **do not swallow.**

As pig's blood is illegal in some states substitute cow's blood.

Some of the recipes in this book are highly stylized. Because we wanted to keep the authenticity of them, we have tried to maintain the 'flavor' of ethnicity within the directions.

Disclaimer for those special readers; you know who you are...

Garlic is used in several of the recipes. It can be easily deleted without substitution and the integrity of the of the dish will remain.

Chapter One
It will have blood-Wm. Shakespeare

Voluptuously the curtains billow in the night air. French windows stand half open as on the bed the unsuspecting maiden sleeps. The wind that moves the curtains gently toys with her dark hair and her breasts, draped in lace, heave in the deep breathing of sleep.

She stirs slightly as if in anticipation, a faint smile plays across her lips. A noise, the creaking of a door, causes her to shift her head to one side.

A shadow that is not a shadow blocks the light of the moon from the balcony and a man who is not a man enters. With the self-assurance of a predator he moves toward the bed. He also smiles in a smirk that reveals a flash of white from between crimson lips.

Silently approaching the bed he closes his eyes and inhales deeply, his head raises almost imperceptibly, as if savoring an intoxicating aroma.

This man who is not a man kneels by the side of the bed as he entwines his hand in the girl's dark tresses. He lays his other hand against her far shoulder and in doing so brushes against her.

The sleeping girl writhes as if in knowing anticipation. He turns her head away from him, exposing her alabaster neck, a vein pulsing under the translucent skin.

He lowers his head, and with a sudden move, he sinks his long sharp fangs into her neck. A single small drop escapes as he rips into her throat and swallows mouthfuls of warm young blood. The Vampire Dines!

Mention blood as food and most of the modern world would consider it the private reserve of vampires and the odd werewolf. But in reality blood has a long history as a food source for humans.

Early man attributed the essence of life to blood since it was noticed that life would leave the body as the blood drained away. Another early concept was the physical and mental characteristics of a person or animal could be absorbed with the drinking of the subject's blood.

Vampires, being dead, seek the one thing they do not have, life. And where better to find life than in its embodiment, blood.

Nevertheless when it came to food, humans suddenly found blood as an animal product was edible. In hunting societies nothing was wasted and a use was found for blood. One French delicacy was the blood of a newly butchered pig mixed with milk and stirred over an open fire until it cooked into a kind of pudding. This was a special treat for children It survives today in the form of drisheen in Ireland.

The modern western world has largely ignored blood as a foodstuff except for ethnic cooking yet there is a long varied heritage.

During the Victorian era women of culture in England and France would venture to a slaughterhouse, braving the possibility of staining their skirts in order to drink a glass of fresh blood. It was believed to be medicinal. This practice fell out of favor in the late 1890's. Coincidentally, after the publication in 1897 of a certain novel by Bram Stoker called <u>Dracula</u>!

Finding blood to cook with can be a challenge but it is not impossible. In larger cities, Filipino and Vietnamese stores carry it in the rozen food section. a slaughterhouse may be able to supply it. In some locales pig's blood is illegal and cow's blood should be substituted. The advantage of the markets is that it is already mixed with anti-coagulants.

Blood will coagulate if left alone. Commercially sodium citrate is mixed with the blood.

This is a harmless compound that can be purchased over the counter from a pharmacy. A very good ratio is 10 milligrams sodium citrate to 100 milliliter of blood. Vinegar can also be added to stop coagulation.

Salt is sometimes used as a preservative. In lean times the Irish of Derry and Tyrone layer salt with coagulated blood. It is then sliced and saved for food in case of lean times.

It is not recommended that one should collect blood oneself, there is the possibility of contamination and disease. However blood itself is nutritious. Four tablespoons of blood contain as much iron and minerals, especially potassium and phosphorus, as ten chicken eggs and has traces of vitamins A, C, and B with one percent glucose. Blood is rich in protein and contains some fat.

In the search for interesting food and interesting people one travels to many exotic places. One very intriguing locale is Transylvania. On a journey what would one find there? Journey with us back through time and find out!

Chapter Two

Breakfast and Brunch: Start your night out right.

Ah, sundown, looks like a lovely morning. (Stretch, yawn, creak of lid) What... oh hello there! I didn't realize anybody was watching. What's that you say? You're here on an investigation?

Oh I see...the rumors we vampires swoop down on innocent victims, tearing out their throats and gorging on their blood. Really, you can be assured, except for maybe a few backwoods cousins in the Carpathians, we really are quite civilized.

Now, don't get nervous, you are right of course, we ARE in the Carpathians, but you are safe here in this castle for tonight. Did you know that your ancestors probably drank blood? Oh yes, well...perhaps not exactly drank but certainly cooked with it.

But how could I know this without knowing your nationality, you ask? Come now, it really doesn't matter all that much. Almost all the people in the world at one time or another cooked with blood.

Mm, I can see you doubt me. Perhaps if you were shown proof. Let me take you down to the kitchens. There I will introduce you to the head of my kitchen, and perhaps she can convince you.

There you will see recipes from around the world which have been able to bring us out of the dark ages. Perhaps there will even be a recipe from your ancestors.

Yes, you shall meet our lovely cook, Rodika, and she is probably preparing some breakfast even as we speak, perhaps even the lunches are ready. Oh yes, the cooks are constantly busy, after all there really isn't much to do in these dark woods, and we do still so love to have something to bite, I mean, of course, to eat.

Shall we descend...

VERILETUT

Blood Pancakes

- 1 small onion, chopped
- 1 tablespoon butter
- 1 1/2 cups fresh blood
- 1 1/2 cups light beer
- 1/3 cup rye flour
- 1/3 cup barley flour
- 1 egg
- 2 tablespoons sea salt (or to taste)
- 1/4 teaspoon white pepper (or to taste)
- 1/2 teaspoon marjoram, crushed
- 2-3 teaspoons oil

Brown the onion in the butter and let it cool. Pour the blood into a mixing bowl through a sieve. Beat it for a while with a wire whisk until thin strings form and the blood turns lighter in color. Add the beer, and beat. Add the fried onion, rye flour, barley flour, and egg, beating well to keep the batter smooth. Add salt, pepper and marjoram.

Heat a pancake pan with small rings, and grease the rings. Pour them about 2/3 full of batter, and fry the pancakes on both sides until crisp and brown. Keep warm until served. Excellent with lingonberry or cranberry preserves.

FINLAND

FRITKATZA

Scrambled Blood and Eggs

Blood and intestines of one lamb
Onion
Eggs

The lamb's blood is collected upon the butchering of the animal and coagulates in a mold for cooking. The intestines are cooked and cut up.

The blood, also cut up, is fried with onion and the intestines. It is then added to the beaten eggs.

In Basque cooking there exists a link between blood and the intestines that is clearly seen in this recipe. The intestines of a suckling lamb are not strong enough for stuffing. This is a typical spring meal, spring being the best season for suckling lamb.

BASQUE

BLACK BREAKFAST

     Intestines or skins in suitable lengths
3 1/8 quarts blood
    3 pounds onions, chopped (about 10 1/2 cups)
    3 pounds pork fat, leaf lard for preference
    3 cups heavy cream (or evaporated milk)
1 1/2 cups bread crumbs
    6 tablespoons course salt
    1 teaspoon quatre-épices or other spices
    1 teaspoon of sugar (preferably brown)
    Chopped parsley, chives or sage- to taste
  1/4 cup rum (optional)

Put the bread crumbs to soak in the cream. Add the seasoning to the blood.

Cut the fat into small dice, and try out about 1/2 pound in a heavy frying pan. When the lard runs out, add the chopped onions and cook them slowly without allowing them to catch. They should melt rather than fry.

When they are ready mix in the rest of the fat, which has been diced, and the cream and bread-crumb mixture. Stir it well together and pour in the blood still stirring. Finish according to basic method.

FRANCE

PUDDING CAKES

Mix blood and cooked rice, season to taste. Form into patties and bake.

INDONESIA (Celebes and Sulawesi)

Vietnam: A nameless entity, it has long red insect-like antennae as a nose and uses this to suck with. At times existing only as a disembodied head, decapitation does no good and it has no body to destroy.

BLODPØLSE

Hot Bloodmeal Cereal

- 1 pint milk
- 1 pint water
- 5 tablespoons sugar
- 1/2 teaspoon ginger
- 1/2 teaspoon powdered cloves
- 1 teaspoon salt
- 1 cup rice
- 1/2 cup pearl barley
- 2 pints fresh blood
- 1 tablespoon bread crumbs
- Melted butter Powdered sugar

Add sugar, ginger, cloves, and salt to milk and water. Add rice and barley and cook until mixture begins to thicken.

Add blood that has been beaten with a wire whisk and bread crumbs.

Fill greased baking tins, place them in a pan of hot water, and bake for about 2 hours in a 275 to 300 degree oven. Slice while warm and serve bloodmeal cereal with melted butter and powdered sugar.

NORWAY

BLOOD BREAKFAST CAKES

Thicken cow's blood with fine oatmeal and season to taste. Shape into patties and fry.

SCOTLAND

BOUDINS NOIRS

- 1   pound of blood
- 1   pound of onions
- 1   pound leaf lard
- 2/3   pounds apple marmalade
- 1/3   pint cream Chopped parsley Salt Pepper Allspice Nutmeg Celery Savory

Chop up onions. Put 1 ounce lard in a saucepan with the onions, and leave to cook over a low fire for about an hour. Stir from time to time. Remove the skin from the leaf lard, and cut up into quarter inch squares. Put these into a colander and plunge it for 5 minutes into boiling water, being careful to keep the pieces detached.

Drain for a few moments without pressing. Put this lard in with the onions, when the latter are well cooked, and stir until thoroughly mixed. This should be done on a very slow fire.

Pour in the blood, straining it through a fine sieve to suppress any coagulated parts. Mix all well, adding the apple marmalade. Season with spices to taste.

Keep warm while filling casings. Cook using standard instructions.

FRANCE

Vlad Dracula (1431-1476) was a Wallachian Prince who, by alliances and military actions, attempted to save what is now Romania from Turkish invaders. Reviled by his enemies and revered by his countrymen as a national hero (especially after his death), he caused thousands to be massacred by impalement thus earning the name Vlad Tepes or Vlad the Impaler. Bram Stoker used him as a source for his novel, <u>Dracula</u>.

Though at times accused of cannibalism and blood-drinking there is no historical proof of such. He was believed to have been killed by his own men by mistake as he returned from a spying mission against the Turks. A mystery surrounds his burial which may be in the floor of a monastery at Snagov.

Chapter Three

Midnight Delight: Those between meal snacks.

Why, look how time always flies in my kitchen. See...the moon is directly overhead!

Tsk, Tsk...! You look a little pale. Ah, what you need is a little snack. You must be starved, after watching us make those tasty morning meals. Ach, how rude of old Rodika not to have offered you any. Why did you not ask for a sample? Such a way to treat a guest.

We need to make a little something to get rid of the little churning in the stomach. Yes, and to put you in a cheerful humour.

Ah...old Rodika make joke! Blood was considered to be one of the four cardinal humours, or liquids in the body, and was responsible for cheerfulness, optimism, and confidence. There were really quite a few peoples who used blood nourishment as a quick pick-me-up.

For instance, Arabs before the coming of Islam would mix camel hair and blood and cook it over a fire, and the Berbers have been known to open the veins of cattle and either drink the blood fresh or mix it with milk.

The Patzinak tribes opened veins in their horses necks if they were thirsty and no water was available.

So did the Masai of Tanzania, except they had honed it to a finer art. These people have an arrow which has a stop below the point to prevent it from penetrating too far into the neck. Simply, the Masai would then drain off as much blood as they wanted and then would close the wound with a plug. We have similar spigots in the blood barrels which are in the dungeons.

Oh my, that may have been misleading...the barrels contain wine, but, of course, only Bulls Blood wine called Egri Bikaver, from the Eger region north of Hungary. What's that you ask? Why, yes this really can be sustaining, and useful too.

Marco Polo reported that the Mongols on long journeys would drink the blood of their horses for nourishment. Each man with a string of eighteen horses, allowing for frequent mount changes, would take a little over one-half pint from the vein of a horse daily. This little bit, compared to a horse's weight, did not harm the horses, and sustained the Mongols on their long and arduous journeys.

But enough such talk. Old Rodika loves to ramble. Let us get you a snack worthy of the master's guest. Most of these delicacies, feel free to pick up and sample as we wander amongst the tables, for most of these are served at what is called 'Blood Heat'. This means these delicacies are at a body temperature of 98.6 degrees Fahrenheit, or thirty-seven degrees Celsius. Food at this temperature will feel lukewarm when you pick it up. Come this way...

VAMPIRE IN A COFFIN

SAUCISSE EN CROUTE

- 1 cup unbleached all-purpose flour
- 1/4 teaspoon salt
- 4 tablespoons unsalted butter, cut into small pieces
- 1/4 cup water
- 1 egg, lightly beaten with 1 tablespoon water
- 1 3/4 pound blood sausage (about 1-2" wide) preferably garlic or pistachio

Stir together flour and salt until well mixed. Add the butter and mix with your fingers until the mixture is the texture of bread crumbs. Sprinkle with water and mix well with your hands.

Turn the dough unto a cutting board and gather it into a ball. Work the dough by pressing a little away from the rest and then more and more until a new ball is formed, ensuring the butter gets worked evenly throughout the dough.

This can also be done step by step with a food processor, or if you prefer, frozen pastries will do just fine.

Refrigerate in waxed paper until ready for use.

Prick the sausage with a fork, place in a skillet with water to cover. Bring to boil, then reduce heat to low, simmer for ten minutes if 1" across, twenty minutes if its 2" across.

Preheat oven to 350 degrees F. Remove dough and roll out until about 1/8" thick. The size should be so you can roll the sausage up completely in the dough. Seal it well, including the ends, by crimping.

Place seam-side down on a non-stick baking sheet. Bake for 45 minutes or until brown all over. Serve hot or warm but cut with a serrated knife so as not to crush the dough.

Serves 4 as an appetizer.

FRANCE

> France: The fifteenth century Marshall of France, Gilles de Rais, was a suspected child molester and fought alongside Joan of Arc in her campaigns against the British. Little known is he suffered from haemotomania, literally, a lust for blood. In the throes of this madness he is said to have murdered hundreds of children earning the nickname of the Black Baron; he was executed in 1440.

NUER ROASTS

The Nuer tribe of the Upper Nile in Africa bring to us some basic cooking.

Generally they treat blood in two ways.

One method is to boil the blood basically to thicken it, and drink it like a thick broth.

Another method is to allow the blood to coagulate into lumps which can then be roasted in the embers of fire, sort of like roasting marshmallows.

NORTH EAST AFRICA

Africa: In the Ashantiland, anyone can become an Asanbosam by sucking the blood of a sleeper.

In Guinea there is the the Owenga.
In the Herrerosland, the Otgiruru, looks like a dog, and can kill who answers its call.

In the Loango the Vampire lies with its eyes open while at rest and the moon can give it up to ten times its strength. It moans if burned, and can turn itself into a bat.

Ex-sorcerers become this creature, and to be destroyed it must be burned on the night of a full moon. Even the tinest unburnt partical can rejuvinate back into the original creature.

Italy: Italy, though not particularely known for Vampires in modern times has had blood drinkers Gaetano Mammore, an infamous brigand, drank the blood of victims and enemies to steal their life power.

Nearby, in Sardinia, the concept of vendetta caused many deaths. It was believed the spirit of a murder victim could not rest until vengeance had been taken by a family member upon the killer or his family.

CROSTINI

Liver Pate

Celery
Carrots
Parsley
Olive oil
Chicken livers
Blood
Tomatoes
Onion
Anchovy filets
Capers
Salt

Brown a small amount of finely chopped celery, carrots and parsley in olive oil. Then add equal amounts of blood, chopped chicken liver and chopped tomatoes. Cook this mixture for 5 minutes.

Blend in an electric blender with boiled onion, anchovy fillets and capers. Salt to taste. Pack the paste into a serving dish and heat it in a pan of boiling water for 30 minutes. Spread on French bread or crackers.

ITALY

CANAPÉS

Mushroom Duxelles (see below)

3/4	pound blood sausage
1/2	cup clear meat consomme (see soups)
4	teaspoons tomato puree
4	teaspoons Madeira
1/2	cup heavy cream
4	large slices firm bread
	Butter

Prepare the full recipe for Mushroom Duxelles and keep it warm.

Discard the skin of the sausage, and mix with the sausage enough consomme to make a smooth puree. Heat this in a small saucepan, then add the tomato puree, the Madeira, the cream, and lastly the Duxelles. Stir gently and taste for seasoning.

Trim the crusts from the bread. Fry the slices lightly in butter, on each side, then spread them with the sausage mixture. Serve very hot on individual plates, as first course.

Mushroom Duxelles

1/2	pound mushrooms
2	teaspoons butter
	Minced shallot
	Minced onion
	Salt and pepper

Take the mushrooms, clean, wash and mince. Squeeze though cheesecloth or toweling to remove all the water.

Then heat in a small saucepan with the other ingredients and cook for about three minutes or until tender but not browned. Add the mushrooms and cook over low heat until almost dry. Lightly season with salt and pepper.

FRANCE

France: The coming of plague and outbreaks of vampirism have long been linked in France as in other countries. Special fires were lit because it was believed that when lit demons were unable to pass. Fire has always been an enemy of the reanimated corpse, perhaps for its cleansing aspects.

MICE IN CREAM

Here is a tasty morsel from our arctic fiends, er...friends.

        Several fat mice
        Flour
        Ethyl alcohol
        Salt and pepper
        Fat
6-8 cloves

Skin, gut, and wash some fat white mice without removing their heads, but over a bowl so as to collect the blood. Drain the blood. Cover them in a pot with ethyl alcohol and the blood mixed in and marinate for about 2 hours.

Drain the mice, then dredge them thoroughly in a mixture of the flour, salt and pepper, and them fry slowly in the fat for about 5 minutes. Add a cup of alcohol and the cloves, cover, and simmer for 15 minutes. Transfer the mice into the cream sauce, and warm them in it for about 10 minutes before serving.

Since no recipe for cream sauce was found for this region the authors have provided a generic one below. Use this or a favorite mouse souse, er, sauce.

WHITE SAUCE

- 2 tablespoons margarine
- 2 tablespoons all-purpose flour
- Salt and pepper to taste
- 1 cup milk

Heat margarine until melted, stir in flour, salt and pepper, stirring constantly over a low heat. Stir in milk, heat to boiling. Boil and stir for 1 minute.

IMPORTANT: It is recommended when cooking with rodents to use only those specifically bred for food.

USA (Alaska)

Iceland: There is a saga in Iceland of the Eyrbyggia, a family of Vampires who slew eighteen servant of a houshold in the year 1,000.

Greece: In Greece the Vampire has many names. The Bruculaco, has tense, hard and swollon skin. It is commonly called Timpanita, due to the way the creature sounds when hit. It has a resonant voice as well and can scream once a night.

Excommunication creates it, and it will spread plagues and kill any who answer its call, although the Vampire may be answered if one waits for the second call. To destroy, cut off its head and burn it, but if you are in Milo, chop up the head and boil it in wine.

MYMA

- 2   Pounds veal or beef mince
- 1   cup coagulated blood
- 3-4   tablespoons of ouze rigani, salt, pepper
- 2   onions, finely chopped
- 2   eggs
-       A bit of flour
- 1/2   pound of crustless bread soaked in water

Squeeze as much water as possible from the bread. Combine it with the mince, blood and other ingredients except the ouze.

Knead the mixture. Continue kneading while pouring the ouze slowly into it. Allow to stand in a refrigerator for a short while, making sure it is covered with a clean cloth. Then mold into small balls and fry or use as a poultry stuffing.

Myma was used in ancient times but is rarely eaten today. This recipe is included as an example.

GREECE

LES TOASTS SANGUINAIRES

In Belgium there is a quick and easy lunch a person can make when guests drops by unexpectedly. Just take some blood sausage which are kept ready for this very purpose and poach, cool, skin, and the beat with cream and spread on toast. It takes only moments to prepare and your guests will be delighted.

BELGIUM

Belgium: In Belgium eating soul-cakes to appease the dead is common. Baked on November first, to be eaten the following day, they were thought to fortify the dead. The practice travelled and in Dixmude, it is believed a soul is released from Hell for every cake eaten.

HETE BLIKSEM OR DRENTHE

Hot Lightning

2	pounds cooking apples
2	pounds eating apples
4	pounds potatoes, chopped
	Salt
	Ground cloves
3/4	pound blood sausage, cut in thick slices
	Butter

Peel and core the apples and cut them into pieces. Simmer the cooking apples in a little water in a heavy pan for about 20 minutes.

Add the potatoes and eating apples, and cook them all together for about 30 minutes or until they are soft. Mash them with salt and ground cloves.

Fry the slices of blood sausage in butter (very fat sausage needs no butter). Stir the fat into the mash potatoes and apples, and arrange the slices of sausage on top to serve.

Serves 8.

NEDERLANDS

HIMMEL UND ERDE

Heaven and Earth

Pureed potatoes and Apples with Blood Sausages from Switzerland

The Himmel is the apple representing Heaven and the potatoes represent Erde, or Earth

This recipe has the wonderful advantage of being either a tasty breakfast, brunch or appetizer.

- 2 pounds potatoes, peeled, cut into 1/2" cubes
- 1 1/2 pounds crisp and heavenly apples, peeled, cored, and cut into 1/2" cubes
- 2 tablespoons unsalted butter
- 1 pound blood sausage links, poached and thinly sliced
- 1 tablespoon sugar
- 1 teaspoon salt
- 1/4 teaspoon white pepper
- 2 tablespoons unsalted butter at room temperature, diced

Bring a large saucepan of water to a boil, drop in the potatoes and boil for about 25 minutes, adding the (heavenly) apples after the first 10 minutes.

While the apples and the potatoes are boiling, melt the 2 tablespoons butter in a skillet and fry the sausage slices until lightly browned on both sides. Turn off the heat under the skillet, cover it, and let it sit on the burner.

Drain the potatoes and apples (heavenly), then mash or whisk them together with the sugar, salt, pepper, and diced butter until smooth. The whisk attachment of an electric mixer is fine, however, do not use a food processor, since it will turn the mixture to goo.

A couple of ways to serve:

1: The sausage slices laid on top of the potato and apple puree (heavenly).

2: Chop up the fried blood sausage, mix it into the puree, then form it into patties. Press an even layer of bread crumbs onto the patties, place then on a baking sheet, splash with garlic butter and bake for 15 minutes in a preheated 350 degree F. oven. (If for breakfast you may choose to use an alternative to garlic)

See disclaimer notes on garlic anyway, especially if your breakfast is, shall we say, later than usual?!

SWITZERLAND

HIMMEL ON AHD MET BLOOTWOOSCH

Blutwurst with Applesauce and Mashed Potatoes

Here is a similar recipe from the Rhineland, that is perfect for a brunch or midday meal.

- 2 pounds potatoes, peeled
- 2 pounds Granny Smith apples. peeled, cored, and sliced 1/2" thick
- Juice of 1 lemon
- Sugar
- 2 tablespoons butter
- 2 cups hot milk
- Salt and pepper
- 2-3 tablespoons lard
- 4 large onions, halved, cut into thin rounds
- 4 large, thick pieces of blootwoosch (blood sausage)

Cook the potatoes in salted water. Cut the apple slices in half and cook with a few tablespoons of water, the lemon juice, and the sugar until they almost have the consistency of applesauce.

Drain the potatoes and mash coarsely with the butter and hot milk, then mix the applesauce (which should have little bits of apple) with the potatoes, add a little salt and pepper, and keep warm.

In a large skillet heat the lard and saute the onions until golden brown. Remove the skillet and set aside. Quickly sear the blootwoosch pieces in the same skillet (may need to add a bit more lard), then stack them on top of one another on the side in the skillet, and briefly reheat the onion rings in the skillet. Season with a little salt and pepper.

Serve the blootwoosch on a platter with the mashed potatoes-and-apple mixture, garnished with the onion rings.

GERMANY

> Germany: The spirits of the undead who return to prey upon the living are believed to gather at crossroads. Near a graveyard, crossroads are to be avoided. They are also used in the hopes of detaining spirits. It was often down at the junction of several roads where the public gibbet stood, creating another association between the undead and crossroads.
>
> In many districts anaemia, the wasting disease, attacked herds of cattle. As cleansing by fire helped, it was believed Vampires could not cross it.

GROATS-GUT BEULING

- 3 cups barley groats
- 1 quart pig's blood
- 3 nutmegs
- 3/4 loot cloves
- Salt
- Pig's lard
- Pig's intestines

Take groats and add to hot water that is boiling, let it stand to swell until the groats are nicely swollen, then take the blood, heated until lukewarm, pour through a cloth onto the groats until they are completely red. Mix some pig's lard, cloves, salt and nutmeg. Add to groats. Stir well.

Fill intestines very thin so they are only 1/2 full. They will not boil out this way. They have to boil gently for an hour. Some also take a portion of these prepared groats and mash it with finely mashed pig or beef liver, but then it should be spiced and salted a little more and also (the intestines should be) stuffed more.

NEDERLANDS

Chapter Four
Soups and Stews: Pease porridge NOT!

Wasn't that such a tasty sampling of what our kitchens have to offer. Ah, but now the servants prepare the courses to get us through those late cold hours. Nothing like a bowl of hot soup or stew to keep your blood warm, old Rodika always says. Mm, your looking queasy again. Perhaps it is slurping blood with a soup spoon which seems a bit indelicate.

Many peasants from around the world commonly used blood to thicken soups and stews. You began to see in the last chapter we are in historical company.

Ah your eyebrows raise, perhaps we don't seem quite the barbaric creatures your reports told you to investigate after all.

Excuse me for a moment while I check the fires. The other cooks are not always as careful as they need to be. Yes, there's a flame not close enough to the kettle, lets raise it just a bit, there, thank you. You see blood coagulates at 158 degrees Fahrenheit, or seventy degrees Celsius.. Now you can help me check the rest, we must try a taste as we go the rounds...

CZARNINA

Duck Soup

- 1 duck (5 1/2 -6 1/2 pounds) cut up
- 1 quart duck, goose or pork blood
- 1 1/2 pounds pork loin back ribs
- 2 quarts water
- 2 teaspoons salt
- 1 stalk celery
- 1 sprig parsley
- 2 whole allspice
- 2 whole cloves
- 1 pound dried prunes, pitted
- 1/2 cup raisins
- 1 small tart apple, chopped
- 2 tablespoons flour
- 1 tablespoon sugar
- 1 cup whipping cream or dairy sour cream
- Salt, pepper, lemon juice or vinegar

Cover duck and back ribs with water in a large kettle. Add salt. Bring to boiling. Skim off foam

Pour celery, allspice, parsley, and cloves into cheesecloth bag and add to soup. Cover and cook over low heat until meat is tender, about 1 1/2 hours.

Remove spice bag from kettle. Discard bones, cut up meat. Return meat to soup. Add prunes, raisins, and apple; mix. Cook 30 minutes.

With beater, blend flour and sugar into cream until smooth. Then add blood mixture, a little at a time, continuing to beat.

Add about 1/2 cup hot soup stock, to blood mixture, blending thoroughly. Pour mixture slowly into the soup, stirring constantly until soup comes just to boiling.

Season to taste with salt, pepper, and lemon juice or vinegar. Serve with homemade noodles if desired.

For thicker soup increase flour to 3-4 tablespoons or add 1 cup pureed prunes.

POLAND

> Poland: There is a Vampire called the Wieszczy. The male are called Upier and the female, Upiercsa. They are described as having a harelip and a tongue like an insects stinger.
>
> A baby born with teeth signifies a possible victem to this curse. They go out at night tolling bells and calling out the names of villagers who will then die almost at once. When the person dies, bury face down with a cross made from willow under the armpits, chin, and chest. Also, put a little earth from its homestead on the coffin.

CIVET DE LIÉVRE

Jugged Hare

1	young hare
1	hare liver
	Blood from the hare
	Salt and pepper
	Thyme
	Bay Leaf
	Onions
1/2	cup olive oil
1/4	cup brandy
	Bacon
	Butter
	Flour
1	cup red wine
	Bouquet Garni
	Garlic
	Mushrooms
1/2	cup cream
	Croutons

Draw and skin a young hare and save the blood and liver. Cut the body into several pieces, season them with salt, pepper, thyme, and a crushed bay leaf, put them in a bowl, and slice some onions over the meat. Pour over this the oil and brandy, turn the pieces of meat over once to coat well, and then several times more during a 3 to 4 hour period.

Parboil some squares of lean bacon and then brown them in a generous quantity of butter. Remove them from the pan and reserve. Add to the same pan and add some quartered onions. Thoroughly dredge the pieces of hare in flour and fry them in the pan with the onions until they, too, are well browned. Add red wine to cover, a bouquet garni, and a clove of garlic.

Cover the pan and simmer for about 1 hour. Remove the pieces of meat, add the marinade to the cooking pan, then strain this combined marinade and cooking stock and reserve it.

Put the hare in a casserole, add the fried bacon and a number of small onions and small mushrooms that were lightly browned in butter. Pour the strained cooking stock over the hare. Cover the casserole and put in a 350 degree F. oven for 45 minutes.

When the meat is done, add a mixture of the finely chopped hare liver, the blood, and the cream; stir and simmer a few minutes until the sauce thickens. Correct the seasoning and serve garnished with large, heart-shaped croutons.

FRANCE

HARE SOUP

- 1 old hare
- Mace
- Salt
- Onions
- 1 red salted herring
- Mushrooms
- 1 glass red wine
- Barley
- 1/4 pound butter
- 1 pint hare blood

Cut up an old hare into small pieces and put them into an earthenware casserole. Add mace, onions, a red (salted) herring (previously soaked for 8 hours), some mushrooms, a glass or so of red wine, and 3 quarts water. Cook in a 450 degree F. oven for 3 to 4 hours.

Strain the soup and add to it some cooked barley and a quarter pound butter. Thicken the soup with hare blood. Reheat without boiling.

ENGLAND

England: Wheras in most of the world Vampires are gaunt, in this country they are often seen as plump, although sleek and of an unhealthy pallor.

NTSIN

Meat Stew

- 1 quart sheep or goat blood
- Salt
- 1 pounds viscera (liver, lungs, kidneys, heart, brains, tripe, intestines, pancreas
- 1 onion
- Hot peppers (to taste)
- 3 whole tomatoes
- 2 cups boiled rice

Stir salt into the fresh blood to prevent clotting.

Cut viscera into small pieces and wash well. Place in large kettle. Add enough water to cover meat and cook over a brisk heat.

Chop the onions and add them with the whole peppers and whole tomatoes to the pot. Boil until the vegetables are soft. Remove the peppers and tomatoes and grind them into a paste, then return them to the kettle.

Simmer until the meat is tender.

Strain the blood then stir into the ntsin until it thickens.

Serve over boiled rice and with yams.

GHANA

COCIDO MADRILENO O OLLA PODRIDO

Madrid Stew or "Rotten Pot"

- 1 pound chick-peas (garbanzos), soaked overnight
- 1/2 stewing chicken, about 2 pounds
- 1 pig's foot
- 1/2 pound fresh or salted beef stew meat, with bone if possible
- 1/4 pound bacon
- 1/4 pound tocino cut into cubes
- 1 morcilla (black blood sausage)
- 1/4 pound chorizo
- 1 large onion, sliced
- 1/2 small head of cabbage, shredded
- 2 carrots, chopped
- 1/2 head (not clove) garlic
- Salt and pepper

Half fill a large (4 quart) pot with cold water and put in the chick-peas, chicken, pig's foot, beef, bacon, tocino and sausages. Bring to a boil and skim, then simmer half covered on a low heat for 2-3 hours, skimming occasionally. Add more (hot) water if necessary.

Put the prepared vegetables, and the garlic in 1 unpeeled piece in the pot, add more boiling water if necessary, and pepper and salt to taste. Bring back to a boil and simmer for 1 hour at least.

When ready to serve, remove the garlic and throw it away. Remove meats and sausage with a slotted spoon and cut into serving pieces. Pile the chick-peas and vegetables into a large hot dish, arrange the meats and sausages around them and pour a little broth over the top.

The rest of the broth should be served first as soup with either fried bread cubes or pasta added. You can keep the stew hot while eating this, though it is the Spanish custom to let it stand and eat it lukewarm.

This is one of Spain's oldest dishes. It is a very accommodating dish, infinitely stretchable and easy to cook: all you need is a very large pot and a fire of some sort. Some of the ingredients may be left out, if they do not happen to be available. Also it improves with keeping for a day at least and does not easily spoil.

SPAIN

> Spain: El Vampiro! It can fall prey to strange spirits and animates the first corpse it finds thereby taking on all kinds of shapes.

BRUCKFLEISCH

Mixed-Organ Stew

Beef spleen, heart, aorta
Calf's sweetbreads
Beef blood
Onions
Lard
Carrots
Celery root
Garlic
Vinegar
Salt
Pepper
Red wine
Thyme, bay leaf and marjoram
Dumplings

Cut spleen, heart and sweetbreads into small slices. Cut a piece of aorta into rings. Fry finely chopped onions in lard until golden. Add finely chopped carrots, celery root, and garlic and cook a little.

Pour in a little vinegar and add all the meats except the spleen and sweetbreads. Salt and pepper and add a generous amount of red wine and a bouquet garni consisting of thyme, bay leaf and marjoram. Simmer, covered for an hour, add the other meats, and continue to simmer until all are tender. Thicken the stew with blood and serve it with dumplings.

AUSTRIA

Austria: Catalyptic and semi-catalyptic states are fairly common in this country so the incidents of live burial are not uncommon. The Vampires are fairly traditional and this could easily be the cause of many preternatural rumours.

In Austria, as well as Germany cakes are offered to the dead by the living. These cakes are known as 'souls' are made by a specific method. The season of the dead is observed with tremendous honour. According to Montague Summers: "In the villages they believed that as the curfew rings the departed will come back to their old accustomed places round the hearth and two or three chairs are always left vacant in the circle."

POTAGE D'ALOSE

Shad Broth

1/2	bottle of dry red wine per person
	Fresh caught shad
	Salt
	Clove
	French bread
	Garlic
	Pepper

Heat the wine until it is covered with froth but not actually boiling.

The shad should be freshly caught, preferably still alive, and should not be washed or scaled. The head of the fish is cut off over the pan containing the wine because both the blood and the head are essential to the dish.

The broth then is lightly salted and a clove added. Cooking is for no longer than 10 minutes with the stock kept just below the boiling point.

The broth then is strained into a soup tureen or into bowls that contain slices of French bread, some thinly sliced garlic, salt and a generous amount of freshly ground pepper.

FRANCE

DINUGUAN

- 1/2 kilo pork shoulder (kasim), or ham, diced into 1" squares
- 2/3 cups vinegar
- 1 large onion, sliced
- 1/2 teaspoon crushed peppercorns
- Salt
- 3 tablespoons lard
- 6 cloves garlic, pounded
- 1/2 cup pork blood
- 2 cups water
- 2 sprigs oregano
- 1 teaspoon vet-sin
- 2 teaspoons sugar
- 2 tablespoons patis
- 2 large hot peppers

Soak pork in vinegar with onion, pepper, and salt. Set aside.

Saute garlic in lard, put in marinated pork and bring to a boil. Cover and simmer for 30 minutes until pork is tender and the sauce is almost dry. Chop coagulated pork blood and add. Blend well. Add water, oregano, vet-sin, sugar and patis. Drop in hot peppers and simmer for 10 minutes.

Serves 6.

PHILIPPINES

QUICK MEAT CONSOMME

Nice French Stew

- 1/2 pound ground lean beef
- 2 egg whites
- Trimmings from lean beef
- 6 leeks (white parts only)
- 1 celery heart
- 1 onion
- 2 1/2 tablespoons meat extract of finest quality (blood)
- Pinch salt
- 3-4 quarts water

Mix the ground beef with the egg whites. Place these in a 6-7 quart kettle. Add any extra lean beef. Heat in a 400 degree F. oven for a few minutes to extract the fat.

Wash the leeks and celery and cut them into large pieces. Peel the onions, cut in half, and char the cut sides in a hot skillet. Add the vegetables, the meat extract, and the salt to the meat in the kettle, and cover with cold water. Stirring constantly, bring the mixture to the boiling point. Then reduce the heat and simmer, uncovered, for about 1 1/2 hours.

FRANCE

SHWARZ SAUER

Pennsylvania Dutch Black Soup

      Giblets of 1 goose or duck
- 1/4 cup sugar
- 1/2 pound peeled apples or pears
- 4 pepper-corns
- 1 1/2 tablespoons vinegar
- 2 tablespoons flour
- 1/4 pound prunes
- 1 small stick of cinnamon
- 2 cloves
- 1 pint goose or duck blood
- 1 1/2 quarts water

Use neck, head, feet, wings, heart and gizzard of goose or duck, <u>well cleaned</u>. Cook until tender in 1 quart of water with salt, pepper and cloves. Cook the prunes and apples or pears (quartered) in a pint of water.

Stir the blood with the flour into 1/2 of the broth for the giblets, and pour back on again. Add the chopped fruit, then season with vinegar and sugar and bring to a boil, stirring constantly to prevent coagulation.

NEDERLANDS

SVARTSOPPA

Swedish Black Soup

        Giblets of 1 goose
1 3/4 pints water
    1 slice of onion
  1/2 tablespoon salt
    5 white peppercorns
    3 cloves
  3/4 pint goose blood
    4 ounce flour
    3 quarts stock and giblet stock
    2 ounce sugar
  1/2 teaspoon white pepper
  1/2 teaspoon ground ginger
  1/2 teaspoon cloves
       Salt
    7 tablespoons table or wine vinegar
    7 tablespoons brandy
3 1/2 tablespoons red wine

Prepare giblets similar to the last recipe except cooking time will be about 2 hours.

Strain the blood,. Whisk the flour and blood together to form a smooth thickening. Bring the stock and giblet stock to a boil in a large pan. Pour in the thickening whilst beating vigorously and let the soup simmer for about 10 minutes, beating continuously.

Draw aside from the heat and flavor the soup carefully. Spices, wine, and fruit should be added with great care—no single spice should predominate the flavor. The soup is improved by being made the day before it is served.

Heat the soup. Whisk the whole time to prevent curdling.

Serve the soup very hot with the giblets, cut into cubes, slices of goose liver sausage and fresh fruit.

The accompaniments can be arranged on a separate serving dish or put into the soup plates.

SWEDEN

> Finland: A belief in spirits who cause illness, especially fever and ague, were recruited from the death of murderers, violent deaths, and old maids.

TI SHEH TAN

Chinese Chicken Blood Soup

	Tofu
2	eggs
	Oil
3	cups water
1	cup chicken blood
1	teaspoon vinegar
1	teaspoon soy sauce
	Pinch of pepper

Cut a block of tofu into thin strips 1 inch long. Fry a well beaten egg in oil as a very thin omelet. Prepare a second omelet and cut both into very thin strips. Boil water, add blood, and simmer for 1 minute.

Remove the coagulated blood and cut into thin 1 inch strips. Reboil water, add the tofu and coagulated blood, and simmer for 10 minutes. Add the eggs, vinegar, soy sauce, and a pinch of pepper.

This interesting Chinese soup uses three coagulated proteins. The blood, eggs and soybean create a colorful delight as well as a tasty soup with interesting texture.

CHINA

China: The Ch'ling Shih has burning red eyes, long, curved, claw-like nails and a greenish-white hue with long hair. It can fly fast and gets its flying strength from the moonlight.

If burnt it will shriek. To be laid to rest, lay a circle of rice grain around it and thread seven pieces of jujube on its backbone.

CIVET DE MOU DE VEAU

Calf Lung Stew

	Lungs from 2 calves
1	pint calf's blood
	Salt and pepper
	Flour
	Butter
1	pint dry red wine
	Bouquet garni
1	clove garlic
2	strips bacon
	Carrots
	Onions
	Mushrooms
	Croutons

Salt and pepper pieces of lungs and fry them in butter until well browned. Sprinkle with flour, stir well, and cook for a few minutes thickening with blood. Cover with dry red wine.

Add a bouquet garni and some crushed garlic. cover and bake in a moderate oven for 1-1/2 hours. Transfer the pieces of lung to a shallow baking dish and add some chopped and fried bacon, sliced or whole mushrooms, and a number of small onions and carrots fried in butter or with the lean bacon.

Cover with the strained cooking liquid and return to the oven for an additional 30 minutes. Garnish with croutons.

FRANCE

Chapter Five

Main Dishes: Abandon hope all who Entree here

As you can see, being head cook does have its delicious advantages. But old Rodika hopes you saved room for the main courses.

First, we'll explore many of the possibilities which show how creative cooks have been, and indeed, can be. Keep in mind there are a whole slew of puddings and sausages, but we will get to those in later chapters of this adventure.

Here, there are a few...curious recipes to be gleaned, but do not be put off, many types of blood, are used in cooking. Although, as you have seen mostly cow and pig blood. There even are some places that use dog's blood. Certainly in Hawaii, the brains and blood of dogs were eaten, and it is rumored that the Samoans probably consumed dog's blood as well.

It is more economical to use the cow or pig, but old Rodika supposes, one must use what one has in the backyard. How is it more economical? You see, káposzia, an adult hog yields up to five to ten pounds of blood, and an adult steer can supply up to thirty to forty pounds of blood. Oh yes, and then there are sheep, but they only supply about three to five pounds of blood per adult.

Lean closer, let old Rodika whisper you a secret: from these animals really only the first two pounds of blood are the best. That is why old Rodika is the head cook, but please, don't put this in your investigation.

Here is another secret of the cooks of the master's kitchens. We borrowed this from the Tibetans. If the animal is killed by suffocation, all the blood will stay in the meat. What? You're correct of course, but even though the Tibetans have such dietary restrictions there is a dish call "gyuma" for which beef is acceptable. Alas, it sounds like it might be delicious, but we have only recently unearthed the recipe and I have not tasted it yet. Perhaps if you visit us again.

Oh my, listen how old Rodika can digress! You were told about the regions that use dog's blood to whet your appetite for some of the more exotic repasts you are about to enjoy. Just over here...

LAMPROIE À LA BORDELAISE

Lampreys

A whole Lamprey
Onion
Carrots
Salt and pepper
Butter
A clove garlic
Bouquet garni
Red Bordeaux wine
Leek, sliced
Bacon
Butter and flour roux
Croutons

Reserve the blood from the lamprey. Cut the fish into thick slices and place them in a pan on a bed of lightly sauteed sliced onions and carrots. Salt and pepper. Add garlic and bouquet garni and enough red Bordeaux wine to just cover the fish.

Boil rapidly for 10 to 15 minutes and then remove the slices of lamprey. In a shallow casserole alternate the lamprey and some sliced leeks sauteed in butter with chopped bacon. Prepare a sauce from the strained stock and a light butter and flour roux.

Strain this sauce over the fish and simmer it until done. Remove from the heat, carefully stir in the reserved blood, and garnish with large triangular croutons.

FRANCE

FILETS DE LIEVRE À LA PROVENCALE

Hare Fillets Provence Style

Hare fillets
Anchovy fillets
Salt
Pepper
Crushed garlic
Bacon
Olive oil
Tomato paste
White wine
Bouillon
Hare blood

Lard fillets of hare with rinsed anchovy fillets. Sprinkle with salt, pepper, and crushed garlic, wrap in bacon, and cook in a covered pan with a little olive oil for about 45 minutes, basting occasionally.

Remove the meat and prepare a sauce by blending into the pan juices some tomato paste, white wine, and bouillon thickened with hare's blood.

FRANCE (Provence)

BLOOD LOAF

1	pound desalted salt pork, diced
2	cups finely chopped yellow onion
1/2	stick margarine
1	pound white yam, peeled and grated
1	pound calabaza, peeled and grated
1/4	cup snipped Spanish thyme or 1 table spoon dried thyme leaves
1	tablespoon dried marjoram leaves
1	teaspoon grated or ground cloves
1	teaspoon freshly grated nutmeg
	Juice of 1/2 lemon
1/2	chili pepper, seeded and forced through a garlic press
1/2	teaspoon freshly ground black pepper
1/2	teaspoon salt
2	cups pig's blood

Thoroughly mix all the ingredients into a large bowl. Meanwhile, oil a bread-pan and preheat the oven to 250-300 degrees F.

Divide the contents into equal amounts for processing. Process each for 6-10 seconds.

As each blot is finished, pack it into the bread pan. When finished, smooth surface and cover with aluminum foil.

Bake for 40 minutes, remove foil, bake for another ten minutes.

Remove from the oven and pour off any excess liquid.

Cut into 1" thick slices, and then into 1" thick strips. Fry gently in margarine until lightly brown. Serve.

CARIBBEAN

BEEF MEAT COVERED WITH BLOOD

      Slab of beef on a bone
      Mixture of salt, cloves, lemon peel, marjoram, and pepper, to taste
      Bacon
2   cups blood
      Wine mixture consisting of 1 part wine, 1 part vinegar and 2 parts water

Cut from the bone a piece of good beef. Pound the beef well and rub it with the mixture. Let stand over night. In the morning, remove the excess salt.

Cook some diced bacon in a large roasting pan and place the beef on top of it. Cook for about fifteen minutes. Smother the beef with blood and continue to roast while basting with same.

When the outside of the beef becomes crusty, pour on the wine mixture. Cover with a wet paper, and braise for three hours. Serve gravy (of course!) with meat.

This is actually from the 1826 cooking volume of the Palatinate-Viceroy of what was then Nadorispan (Hungary).

HUNGARY

Hungary: The Vampire is called Farkaskoldus and when dying takes on the aspect of a werewolf.

TACOS DE MORONGA

Blood Sausage Tacos

- 3 tablespoons lard
- 1 pound Moronga Mexiquense, roughly chopped, skin optional
- 12 4-inch warm corn tortillas
- 6 tablespoons finely chopped white onion
- 6 tablespoons roughly chopped cilantro

Fry the Moronga over a very low heat in the lard, stirring from time to time, until the fat pieces in the sausage are slightly golden and exuding their lard—about 10 minutes.

Place a good 2 tablespoons of the Moronga across the tortilla, sprinkle with a little onion and cilantro, roll up loosely, and eat immediately. This is a pan to mouth food.

MEXICO

Mexico: The vampire got the name of 'Honourable Mother' or Ciuateteo because it produces infantile paralysis. It can fly and its limbs and face are painted white. Still-born babies become this creature and the only way to appease them is to offer them bread or meteorites.

Another set of Mexican vampires are the 'Lord of the Mictlampa' and 'Mictecaciuatl Lady of the Place of Death'. They are seen as having a blackened bodies and a skull for the heads.

MORONGA EN SALSA VERDE

Blood Sausage in Green Sauce

- 3 tablespoons lard
- 1 pound Moronga Mexiquense, cut into 1/2 inch slices
- 3 tablespoons finely chopped white onion
- 2 cups salsa de tomate verde, cocida
- Sea salt to taste

Cook the Moronga in the lard over a gentle heat until well browned on the bottom - about 5 minutes. Turn the slices over, add the onion, and continue frying and shaking the pan until browned on the second side - another 3-4 minutes. The onion ought to remain translucent and not brown.

Stir in the sauce, salt to taste, and reduce over a fairly high heat, shaking the pan and scraping the bottom to prevent sticking - about 5 minutes. The sauce should be of a medium consistency and lightly coat the back of a wooden spoon.

Traditionally served with just corn tortillas, it may be used in burritos, tostadas, over tacos, etc.

SALSA DE TOMATE VERDE COCIDA

Cooked Green Tomato Sauce

- 1 pound (about 22 medium) tomate verde, rinsed, husks removed
- 4 chiles serranos
- 2 tablespoons roughly chopped cilantro
- 1 garlic clove, peeled and roughly chopped
- 1 1/2 tablespoons safflower oil
- Sea salt to taste

Put the tomate verde and fresh chiles into a pan, cover with water, and bring to a simmer; continue cooking until the tomate verde is soft but not falling apart—about 10 minutes, depending on size. Remove from heat. Strain, reserving 1/3 cup of the cooking water.

Put the reserved cooking water into a blender jar, add chiles, cilantro, and garlic, and blend until almost smooth. Add the tomate verde and blend for 10 seconds, no more, to make a fairly smooth sauce.

Heat the oil in a frying pan. Add the sauce and reduce over high heat until it thickens and seasons—about 8 minutes. Add salt to taste.

MEXICO

TOLTOTT MALAC GYOMOR
Stuffed Pigs's Stomach

1	pig's head
	Pork skin
2	pounds Pork fat
2	more pig's tongues
3	pig's knuckles
1	pint pig's blood
	Salt and pepper
	Paprika
2	pieces garlic
2	pig's stomachs

In a kettle containing salted water boil for at least 2 hours the head, some pork skin, the pork fat, the extra tongues and the knuckles. Remove the meat from the bones and cut it into 1 inch cubes. Put the skin through a food chopper and mix it with the meat.

Add the blood and enough fat from the surface of the cooking stock to make a moist and soft mixture. Season with salt, pepper, paprika and crushed garlic. Stuff this mixture into the stomachs, sew up the openings and then simmer just below the boiling point for about 2 1/2 hours.

Drain the stomachs, prick them in several places, place a lightly weighted board on top of them, and allow it to cool. Instead of simmering, the stuffed stomachs also may be smoked.

HUNGARY

PATAGONIAN PARILLADA MIXTA

Patagonian Mixed Grill

      Olive oil as needed
- 6 blood sausages
- 6 beef short ribs
- 6 small pieces of fryer or broiler chicken
- 18-24 ounces thick tender steak such as sirloin
- 6 small loin lamb chops (2-3 ounces each) or flank steak
- 12-18 ounces sweetbreads, soaked, blanched and pressed
- 12-18 ounces calf liver
- 6 veal kidneys
- 12-18 ounces spleen, drained, rinsed, and cut into strips about 1 inch wide
- 2-3 tablespoons dried oregano

Salt and perper to taste

Oil grill and place about four inches from heat source. Heat charcoal until starting to turn white. Prick sausages in several places with fork. Lightly sprinkle meats with oregano and brush with a light coat of olive oil.

Place short ribs on grill first, rib side down. Grill for ten minutes, turn, brush with oil, sprinkle with salt and pepper, and grill about thirty minutes longer.

Six minutes after turning short ribs, add chicken to the grill. Chicken will take about ten minutes per side. Brush with oil and sprinkle after turning.

Two minutes after turning chicken, add sausages and cook about 5 minutes per side. Immediately after turning sausages, add other meats and sweetbreads.

Cooking these about 3 minutes on first side. Turn, brush with oil, sprinkle, and cook about 2 minutes on second side.

Serve with spicey dipping sauce.

SPICEY DIPPING SAUCE

- 1/4 cup olive oil
- 1 cup red wine vinegar
- 3 tablespoons cayenne pepper
- 4 cloves garlic, peeled and crushed
- 1 teaspoon freshly ground black pepper
- 1 teaspoon dried oregano leaves, crumbled
- 1/2 teaspoon salt
- 1/4 cup minced parsley

Whisk all ingredients together. Let stand at room temperature overnight (or for at least two hours) to mellow, or refridgerate for several days.

Serve at room temperature.

ARGENTINA

TOTOGA

Roasted Pig Organs

Banana leaves or soaked corn husks
Salt
Breadfruit leaves or wet burlap
Pig:
  Spleen
  Heart
  Lungs
  Kidneys
  Coagulated Blood

Cut meat into small pieces, mix with coagulated blood and salt. Wrap in banana leaves or soaked corn husks. Cover with breadfruit leaves or wet burlap and bake in a ground oven.

SAMOA

Tonga: One way to appease the dead was to offer sacrifices. Often the best sacrifice was the finger joint to many cultures. In Tonga this was also the case. To speed the recovery of a sick relative a portion of the little finger was severed and offered up.

POULET AU SANG

French Style Chicken in Blood Sauce

      Chicken
      Red wine
12   small onions
      Equal amount of squared bacon (to the onions)
12   button mushrooms
      Flour
      Beef bullion cube
      Bouquet garni
      Brandy
      Croutons

Kill a chicken and collect its blood. Mix 2-3 tablespoons red wine with the blood. Cut up the plucked and drawn bird and fry the pieces in butter. Remove the chicken and in the same pan cook lightly the onions, bacon and mushrooms, remove from pan.

Add flour to pan, mix well and cook slightly. Stir in 2 cups red wine and the beef bullion. Cook a bit, then strain. Return the chicken and garnishes to the pan, add a bouquet garni and the strained sauce, cover and simmer for about 45 minutes.

Before serving, stir the blood and wine to thicken the stock. Add some warm brandy and ignite. May be served with croutons.

FRANCE

YRCHINS

Sea Yrchins

2 small pig stomachs
  Well seasoned pork sausage meat
      (enough to stuff the stomachs)
  Several bacon strips
  Almond slivers
  Egg
  Flour
  Pig blood
  Chopped parsley

Stuff the cleaned stomachs with the sausage meat and sew them up. Drape with bacon and slowly roast with frequent basting. Insert almond sliver all over the stomachs (so that they look like a hedgehog or sea yrchin).

Carefully ladle over all a thick batter of egg, flour and pig's blood, and return the stomachs to the oven to brown well. Sprinkle these "yrchins" with chopped parsley and serve.

ENGLAND

TERRAPIN

Turtle

Several Terrapins
Flour
Salt
Cayenne pepper
Black pepper
Mace
Brandy
A cup of Sherry
Heavy cream
Butter
Peeled Terrapin eggs
Butter and flour roux

Decapitate the terrapins, saving the blood. Cut up the meat and liver and mix with the blood. Sprinkle this with flour and simmer in a little water for about 10 minutes.

Add salt, cayenne pepper, black pepper, mace, some brandy and sherry. Simmer until the meat is tender; add heavy cream and a generous amount of butter. Add the peeled terrapin eggs and thicken further, if required with a butter and flour roux.

USA (Ozarks)

DRISHEEN

Black Pudding in County Cork

It is larger in diameter than traditional black pudding.
Traditionally made from sheep's blood.
Tipperary often used turkey or goose blood.

It is made from two parts blood (well salted to keep it liquid) to one part cream or full-cream milk, mixed together with a handful of breadcrumbs or oatmeal, pepper, a pinch of mace and a pinch of nutmeg or thyme. When made at home, and sausage casings are not available, the mixture is poured into bowls and either steamed or cooked in another pan of water in a moderate oven (300 degrees F. electric; gas regulo 3) for about 1 hour. It can be eaten warm or left to get cold. Then it is sliced and either fried or grilled, for breakfast or supper, often with bacon, eggs and sausages.

IRELAND (Cork Market, c. 1900)

Ireland: This Irish creature is called the Dearg-dul and the only way to stop it from coming into existence is to pile large quantities of heavy stones on its tomb.

Countess Erzebet Bathory (1560-11614), a distant cousin of Vlad Dracula, murdered over 650 girls for their blood. She believed bathing in blood would rejuvenate her skin. She was both vain and powerful. Bathory would kidnap girls to her castles or her house on Blutgasse in Vienna to cut them or puncture them with large needles, collecting their blood to bathe in.

When finally caught, her servants were executed and she was walled up in a bedroom of her one of her castles with no human contact. Food was pushed to her through a hole in the doorway's brickwork. She lived for almost four years this way and died at the age of fifty-four.

Carpathian Mountains: The Mahr are the Vampire moths who would swoop down on their victims and feed on their souls. This they would do to those unfortunate enough to have been once bitten.

There are two ways to kill this creature. The first is to drive a wooden stake through its heart which returns the soul to its rightful vessel. The second is to find the moths' lair and expose it to the daylight.

Chapter Six

Puddings: Pudding on the Grits.

Puddins a'hot, a'hot,
Pipin' hot, pipin' hot!
Hot or cold, they must be sold,
Puddins a'hot, a'hot!

Oops! Back already? You caught old Rodika singing to herself while she stirs these puddings. Actually, that was an Old Edinburgh street cry.

Hopefully you're enjoying your tour of the castle kitchens, good! The next items to please your palate are the puddings. Now there is some confusion about what makes a pudding and what makes a sausage, which you shall see.

Here in these kitchens, we cooks came together, and, after much deliberation, came up with the castle policy of how the two shall be defined, at least within our domain.

We decided the puddings shall be those which are creamy and sweet. These are the recipes which contain cream, fruit, raisins, nuts, and other such items which are so hard to keep from sampling as we prepare the servings. The sausages will come later, but we consider those the recipes which contain the heavier portions of meats and seasonings to make them spicy.

    Again as we delve into the spread to follow we are in good company. The Princess Palatine of Louis XIV said, "No one is surprised if I eat blood pudding with pleasure. I have so accustomed my German belly to German dishes that I cannot bear to eat a single French ragout." Let us try these tables...

BLOOD FROM A SCOT'S KITCHEN

Actually this and the next two are Scottish blood puddings.

Ox Blood (or pig's)
Milk
Suet
Oatmeal
Onions
Salt and pepper

Let the blood run into a deep pan; take your time, enjoy it; stirring as you do so, and when it gets a little cold, throw in a little salt, allowing a large teaspoonful for every quart. Push it through cheesecloth.

To each quart of blood add a half pint of milk; stir them together and add, again to each quart, a pound of shred suet, a large handful of oatmeal, and plenty of minced onions, salt and pepper. Cook for half and hour in a double boiler after the water is already boiling.

SCOTLAND

Scotland: Although not specifically a Vampire, the following case often comes up in such discussions. Sawney Bean, an Edinburgh peasant, who with a clan of forty-eight ravaged the Scottish countryside in the fifteenth century.

They lived in a remote cave and devoured those travelling alone. They were executed in 1435 and apparently remained dead.

LAMB'S BLOOD PUDDING

Lamb's blood is considered (by the Scots at least) to be the sweetest blood of all!

Blood
Cream
Salt
Spice
Mint
Chives _or_ young onions, minced small
Fat

Take as much blood as with half a munchkin of cream will fill an ashet; mix the blood and cream together and run through a cheesecloth. Season with salt and spices, a sprig of mint and chives _or_ minced young onions; mince the fat; mix all together and fire in the oven or frying pan.

SCOTLAND

GOOSE-BLOOD PUDDING

Goose blood
Grits
Spice Salt
Sweet herbs
Suet

Chop off the head and save the blood, now also the goose, which you will use for this recipe. Stir the blood until it gets cold, then mix it with grits, spice, salt and sweet herbs, according to fancy, and some beef suet chopped.

Take the skin off the neck, then pull out the windpipe and fat, fill the skin, tie it at both ends, so make a pie of the giblets and lay the pudding in the middle. Bake like a pie.

This pudding is often thickened with barley-meal and cooked in the broth.

SCOTLAND

SPICY CAJUN STYLE BLOOD PUDDING

    4   cups cow's blood
    2   teaspoons salt
 6-10   hot chili peppers
    3   stalks celery
    4   sprigs thyme
  1/4   cup milk
    1   bunch parsley
    2   pounds bread crumbs
    1   pound onions, chives or scallions
  3-4   limes
         Vegetable oil
    2   teaspoons Maggi

Steep the bread crumbs in water. Cut up the chili peppers, removing the seeds, and steep them in milk. Saute the onions, chives, or scallions.

Squeeze the water out of the bread crumbs and feed into a food grinder, alternating with parsley, celery, chilies (removed from milk), onions, chives, or scallions, adding the blood throughout the process.

Remove the stems from the thyme and add. Mix carefully, adding salt. Remember it has to be hot to be authentic. If you taste as you go, remember, do not swallow. Add enough oil to the mixture so it is soft.

Prepare in a casing in simmering water for about thirty minutes (when pricked, no blood should ooze). Peel off casing and serve in bowls.

Yields about 10-20 portions.

USA (Lousiana)

FRENCH BOUDIN

Black Pudding

- 3 large onions
- 1/2 pound raw pork fat
- 3/4 cup pork stock (made from a few bones and a bouquet garni)
- 2 tablespoons lard
- 2 tablespoons flour
- 4 cups scalded rich milk
- 4 cups pig's blood
- 1 teaspoon powdered allspice
- Pinch of powdered cloves
- 1 teaspoon finely chopped parsley
- 1/4 cup brushed mushrooms
- Salt and pepper
- Butter
- 2 finely minced shallots

Grate onions and fat and combine them with stock. Place the mixture into a large saucepan, cover, and bring to a quick boil. Then reduce the flame and bring to a simmer very slowly for at least 1 hour, stirring occasionally.

Blend lard with flour over a low flame and stir in milk, stirring constantly until the sauce begins to bubble. Boil this down to 1/2 its original volume, stirring frequently to prevent scorching. Stir in the onion, pork, fat mixture, bring to a quick boil, lower the flame, and simmer gently for fifteen minutes, stirring almost constantly.

Remove from fire and pour in, all at once, the blood. Add allspice, cloves, parsley, mushrooms and salt and pepper. Cook for 1-2 minutes in a little butter with shallots. Serve hot.

FRANCE

ENGLISH BLACK PUDDING

    5 cups pig's blood
1-1/2 cups bread crumbs
    1 cup suet
    5 cups milk
    1 cup cooked barley
    1 cup dry oatmeal
    1 ounce mint
    Salt and pepper to taste

Mix all ingredients together in a bowl and pour into a large pan and bring to a boil. Pour into a wide shallow bowl and season again if necessary. When cold it may be cut into slices and fried.

Serves approximately 8.

ENGLAND

England: An English fairy tale relates how an old man and his wife had the good fortune to be granted three wishes, be it whatever they chose, gold, jewels, a grand house, any hearts desire. Being very poor they were thrilled and the old man blurted out,"I wish I had a fine black pudding to celebrate this good fortune."

A fine black pudding appeared on the table immediately. The wife became angry that a wish had been wasted and blurted out, "You stupid old man. You think of nothing except your stomach and can see no further than the end of your nose. I wish that pudding were at your nose." And there it instantly appeared as if it had grown there.

Pull as they might, they could not remove it To cut it hurt as if cutting his own nose.

Seeing no recourse he wished the pudding off his nose and though he had neither gold nor jewels he and his wife had a fine black pudding for dinner.

Lilith was said to have been the first wife of Adam made, like Adam, out of the dust of the earth. She considered herself Adam's equal and refused to submit to his will, running away. God sent three angels to bring her back but she would not return. So God made the subservient Eve for Adam and cursed Lilith.

She became a night demon flying through the night to strangle babies and drink their blood. Young men were also her prey as she would come to them while they slept and mate with them to produce demon babies.

The Sumerians called her Kiskil-lilla when they spoke of her in the Epic of Gilgamesh. Babylonian stories called her Lilitu. The owl is sacred to her. She is usually pictured as a beautiful woman with luxurious long hair and wings. Her feet are the talons of a bird.

Chapter Seven

Sausages and more sausages: Links to the past.

Finally we come to the sausages. Let old Rodika tell about the many countries involved in the use of these savory succulents.

First, blood sausages originated in ancient Phoenicia, which is now Lebanon, as a specialty of the hog butchers of Tyre. Pardon? Oh! How did we folks here in the Carpathians come by them?

When the Armenians emigrated to Transylvania they brought with them blood sausage recipes. Then blood sausages became commonplace and enjoyed by both rich and poor after the Crusades. But then, blood sausages have always been the food of the poor in Belgium, Poland and Mother Russia.

Even today, blood sausages are common in northwestern Italy. In Eastern Africa, in the Portuguese areas, people eat them and alsothe west of Finland is famous for their great variety!

My! So many variation! In the Yugoslavian regions, especially Croatia and Slovenia, the popular blood sausages are those flavored in Czech, German and Polish styles. The Romanians like their sausages skinless, like a spicy pudding, and truth be told, take it from old Rodika, skinless sausages are much easier to make, and much less time consuming! Just roll them in bread-crumbs and fry. Cheaper too, since you don't have to get the skins; but the cheapest are the boudin noires as they have the least expensive ingredients. In Bordeaux , on the west coast of Basque country, hot blood sausages are served together with cold oysters.

You see that ancient book on the shelf? It is a very valuable part of the master's collection. It is a cookbook purportedly written by Apicius who was a Roman gourmet and it includes recipes for highly spiced sausages made of blood, many of which we serve the master regularly.

Some of the recipes from that book are so large that they will not even fit into the intestines we normally use. Instead they must be stuffed into animal wombs to serve.

Oh dear, you paled, and we were doing so well, your stomach must be bottomless! Let us get some morsels to hold you over, although old Rodika is sure you will be invited to join the master in a complete meal, he would not have brought you done here just to tease. But for now, just follow over here...

GYUMA

Blood Sausage

- 1 complete set lamb or goat's intestines
- 4 cups rice (or coarsely ground barley or wheat)
- 2 quarts blood
- 2 pounds ground beef (or organs such as heart, liver, kidney, finely chopped)
- 1 cup finely chopped onion
- 1/4 cup finely chopped shallots
- 1 teaspoon finely ground caraway seeds
- 1/2 teaspoon chili powder
- 1/2 teaspoon Szechuan pepper
- Salt to taste

Boil the rice or other grain until half cooked, and set it aside to cool. In a large bowl mix blood, meat, onions and all other spices. Sprinkle with a little flour and mix well. Add the rice to the blood mixture being sure that the rice is not hot. Mix well. This should be relatively runny.

Wash intestines thoroughly.

Tie one end of the intestines with string. Use a plastic funnel or pastry bag with a pipe. Fill intestines. DO NOT OVERSTUFF. Tie the end tightly with string.

Boil at least 2 gallons of water in a kettle. Gently place sausage in boiling water and cook for 5 minutes over a high heat. Prick the sausages with a toothpick in a few places to relieve pressure. Continue to boil for at least 20 minutes more. Prick again deeper with toothpick. If red blood spurts out continue cooking. Serve when no red blood appears when pricked.

TIBET

CAJUN BOUDIN ROUGE

Spicy Blood Sausage

- 1 1/2 pounds pork butt
- 1/2 pound pork back fat
- 2 onions, finely chopped
- 2 tablespoons lard, vegetable oil, or rendered pork fat
- 1 1/2 cup cooked rice
- 2 1/2 cups hog or beefs blood
- 1 cup chopped fresh parsley
- 5 teaspoons salt
- 1 teaspoon ground allspice
- 1 teaspoon ground mace
- 3 tablespoons ground black pepper
- 1/2 teaspoon ground bay leaves (use blender or spice mill)
- 1 tablespoon fresh marjoram or 1 teaspoon dried
- 1 teaspoon dried thyme
- 2 teaspoons red pepper flakes
- 3 cloves garlic, minced
- Medium hog casings

Grind the meat and fat through a 1/4 inch plate. Saute the onions in the lard, oil or fat in a heavy skillet over medium heat until they are transparent. Mix together the ground pork and cooked rice with the blood, parsley, salt, spices, herbs and garlic. Add the cooked onions and stir to combine the mixture evenly. Tie off the end of a 10-12 foot length of medium hog casing and stuff with the mixture. Tie into 4-5 inch links.

Bring large pot of water to just below a simmer. Add the sausages. Keep the heat very low, with the water at about 180 degree F., so the sausages don't burst. Poach the sausages for 30-40 minutes, until you can prick the sausages and no blood comes out, and the internal temperature reads 150 F. You can store the sausages in the refrigerator for 2 or 3 days, loosely wrapped, or freeze them for up to 2 months. To serve, saute them in butter or oil over a low heat.

Makes about four pounds.

USA (Lousiana)

America: Along the slave coast Vampires took the form of the Wume by being the victim of a curse or while having been a criminal while alive.

In the Rocky Mountains, the Vampire has a long flexible snout like an anteater and uses this to suck out the brain through the ear of a sleeping victim.

MORONGA MEXIQUENSE
Mexican Blood Sausage

For boiling while preparing the Moronga:

- 1 small bunch fresh mint
- 8 scallions, with green tops, roughly chopped
- 2 tablespoons sea salt

For the Moronga:

- 8 feet large pork casings, cut into 2 foot lengths
- 2 quarts pig's blood
- 2 tablespoons sea salt
- 1 cup closely packed, finely chopped mint leaves
- 2 cups loosely packed, finely chopped green scallion tops
- 1/2 cup finely chopped white onion
- 1 tablespoon dried oregano, Mexican if possible
- 1/4 cup finely chopped garlic
- 3/4 pound pork fat, cut into strips 1/4 inch square

Approximately 8-9 inch lengths of string for tying

Heat the cooking water in a large pot with mint, scallions and sea salt.

Whisk blood and strain through a cloth. Stir in the rest of the ingredients and using a sausage funnel first put in a strip of fat and then about 1/2 cup of the blood mixture, making sure no greens or fat get stuck along the way. Continue, using a piece of fat every time more blood is added. Be sure to stir for every 1/2 cup or the ingredients may settle at the bottom. Do not overfill the casing or they might burst when cooking. It is generally good to leave about 2 inches unfilled at the end to allow for expansion. Tie another tight knot at the remaining end with more string.

Lifting the Moronga at both ends place gently in the water, which ought to be just starting to simmer. Do not drop the sausage! Keeping the water at a simmer only, cook the narrower casing for about 1 hour and the more bulbous casings for about 1 1/4-1 1/2 hours.

MEXICO

HUTYU

Black Sausage

   Blood, lungs, heart, and spleen of 1 pig (about 200 pounds), cut into 2-inch pieces
5 1/2 pounds pork meat, cut into 3/4-inch pieces
  8 bacon strips, fried and crumbled
   Pig's intestines or sausage casings
  3 pounds rice
 1/2 pound rendered lard
   Pepper, paprika, ground cloves, marjoram, ground dill seeds, and thyme to taste

In a saucepan, heat the pig's blood to a boil. Let cool, and strain through a sieve. Let it settle.

Clean the lungs, heart, and spleen. In a pot with 3 quarts water, boil the lungs heart, spleen and pork meat. Test them with a fork: if it comes out smoothly, the meats are done.

Remove from liquid, let cool, and grind them. Reserve the cooking liquid.

Cook the rice until done in the reserved cooking liquid; save any leftover liquid. Combine the ground meats and rice with the crumbled bacon and 1/3 of the blood.

Mix the remaining blood with any leftover lukewarm cooking liquid and add the spices and herbs. Add salt only if needed, as the blood is already salty.

Combine both mixtures. Stuff the mixture

loosely into the casings. Twist the casings to close, piercing the sausages, with a pin as you go along.

Cook the sausages in simmering water on a low flame for about 20 minutes, or until a greasy liquid spurts out of the sausage when pricked. Remove from water and let cool completely.

Saute the sausages in lard before serving.

ARMENIA

BOUDIN D'AUVERGNE

Black Sausage

3 1/8 quarts blood
  3/4 pound fat hard fat back
  3/4 pound leaf lard
    2 pounds onions, chopped
2 1/2 cups milk
    6 tablespoons salt & pepper
    Quatre-spices to taste

Cut the two sorts of fat into small dice, melt them gently, and add the onions. Cook to a mush. Add to the milk, blood, and seasonings. Finish according to basic method and cook for 1/2 hour.

FRANCE (Auvergne)

Brittany: In Brittany the Vampire is called the Morobondo and assaults cattle. The only way to cure the cattle is to have them pass through a ring of fire.

BOUDIN DE NOEL

Christmas Sausage

  1   pound ground pork
3/4 pint pig's blood
  2   pounds white cabbage
1/2 cups onions, chopped fine
  1   tablespoon salt
1/8 teaspoon pepper

Boil cabbage, then drain and put through a sieve. Mix all ingredients thoroughly over a low heat. Let cool.

Carefully fill the pork casings and tie off. Boil water and add sausages carefully. Prick each sausage carefully with a small pin. Boil until done, pricking to test. If blood oozes from pinprick, sausage is not done.

May be sauteed with apple rings and powdered with brown sugar. The Belgian peasants eat it cold, sliced with well-buttered black bread.

BELGIUM

SALSICCA D'ITALIA

Black Sausage

1 pound lean pork from the neck or shoulder, weighed without bone
1 pound lean veal
1/2 pound hard fat back
1/2 pint pig's blood
2 tablespoons course salt
1 1/2 tablespoons each of ginger, cinnamon, nutmeg
1 heaped teaspoon ground black pepper
2 cups dry white wine

Grind the lean meat; cut the fat into small dice, and add with the blood to the lean. Season. Stir in the white wine and mix everything well. Use either a pig's bladder or large intestine.

Dry for 3 to 5 days, hanging from a hook in an airy, steady temperature of 60 degrees F. Smoke for 4 days over a smoldering fire of juniper branches. Brush over with olive oil and keep in a dry, cold place (40-45 degrees F.), still hanging up.

Leave to mature for at least a month.

NOTE: You can omit the smoking process, and leave the salsicca to continue drying on the hook for 2 months instead of 3-5 days.

ITALY

Ancient Italy: The lamia appeared to be a beautiful woman, but she was in reality a blood drinking half snake creature who attacked men in their sleep and drained them.

KISHKA

    4 quarts blood
    4 pounds beef lard
2 1/4 kasha
  1/2 pound onion
    7 tablespoons course salt
    5 tablespoons black pepper, cayenne, and coriander

Cook the kasha in boiling water. Simmer for 45 minutes. Mix the ingredients and simmer carefully. Pour into tied pig intestines and tie off other end. Boil until pinpricks in intestines do not bleed.

RUSSIA

Russia: There are two types of Russian Vampires. The first is called the Uierczi, and becomes a Vampire through suicide or a violent death, as well as the practice of witchcraft while alive. It can cause draught, even drying up the dew on the plants as it passes by. It can only be killed by drowning in a lake or river, but it may be transfixed by hitting it with a nail, but if a second hit is made, it will be revived.

The other is the Mjertojec. It has a purple face, and is active from midnight until the thrice cock crowing. One may become this Vampire by being the offspring of a witch or werewolf, or by behaving as such during life. Excommunication can also be a cause. To prevent this from happening poppy seeds may be sprinkled from the tomb to the house of the deceased. It can be killed by nailing it through the heart to the coffin or by burning.

BOUDIN NOIR AU CERFEUIL

Blood Pudding Sausage

- 3/4 pounds fatback, cut into 4 pieces
- 4 cups fresh pork blood
- 1 tablespoon finely chopped chervil
- 2 teaspoons salt
- 1/4 teaspoon pepper
- 1/4 teaspoon Pate Spice or Bouquet Garni
- 1 yard sausage casing

Place the fatback in a pot with 8 cups water. Bring to a boil and continue to boil for 20 minutes. Drain in a colander. Allow the fat to cool, then dice into 1/8 inch cubes.

In a bowl mix the fatback with the blood. Add the chopped chervil, salt, pepper, and pate spice. Stir well.

Wash the sausage casings well; inside and out with cold water. Make a knot at one end and tie off with a piece of string. Fill the casings to 2 inches from the top. Twist and tie a knot in the end. Tie off with string.

Place the sausage in a large pot containing 1 gallon of water. Heat the water to 160 degrees F. No bubbles should break the surface of the water-and poach for 15 minutes, occasionally stirring gently with a wooden spoon to maintain an even temperature.

Take a very sharp needle and gently prick any area where large air pockets have formed. This will prevent the casings from popping. Poach for 15 minutes more. Pierce the boudin with the needle. If no blood runs out, the sausage is cooked and should be removed from the water; if the blood is still liquid, poach for a few minutes more.

Cool the boudin completely. With a sharp knife, cut it in 4 to 6 inch sections. Place under a hot broiler for a few minutes or saute in butter until heated through. Boudin is served hot.

FRANCE (Normandy)

KISZKA Z KRWIA

Pig Organ Sausages

- 1 pig snout
- 2 pig's feet, split
- Salt and pepper
- 1/2 pound pork
- 2 pounds pig's liver
- 5 onions
- Peppercorns
- 4 pound course buckwheat grits
- Allspice
- Marjoram
- 2 cups pig's blood
- Butter

Simmer salt feet and pork in salted water containing 1 onion and peppercorns. Scald the liver and add this water to the pork stock. Remove the meat from the bones and grind it and the liver in a meat grinder.

To the stock pot add 4 chopped onions and the grits (previously washed), some crushed allspice and some marjoram and continue cooking until the grits are tender. (Add more water if the mixture becomes too dry.) Salt and pepper to taste.

Remove the pot from the heat and cool. Stir in pig's blood and stuff this mixture into sausage casings. Tie into convenient lengths and simmer the sausages in boiling water for about 20 minutes. Serve cold or hot, the latter by slicing and frying in butter until brown.

POLAND

BOUDIN DE LAPIN

Rabbit Sausages

	Milk
	Bread crumbs
1/2	hard pork fat
1	pound rabbit meat
1/2	pound lean pork
2	eggs
	Rabbit Blood
	Onion
	Shallots
	Butter
1	rabbit liver, minced
	Salt and white pepper
	Cloves
	Cinnamon
	Black pepper
	Nutmeg
	Chopped parsley
	Chives
	Tarragon

Prepare a thick panada by boiling bread crumbs in milk. Allow it to cool. Beat into the panada a mixture of rabbit meat, hard pork fat and lean pork that were well blended in an electric blender with the eggs.

Fry some finely chopped onions and shallots in butter until they are wilted, mix in the minced rabbit liver and a little rabbit blood, and cook gently for a few minutes.

Add this onion-blood mixture to the meat-panada, season with salt, white pepper, black pepper, nutmeg, cloves, cinnamon, chopped parsley, chives, and tarragon and knead well with the hands. Stuff into rounds and pouch.

FRANCE

BUZKANTZAK

Blood Sausages

   13 pounds onions, not sweet
   18 large leeks, white part only
4 1/2 pounds fat from the kidney and
         peritoneum, or lard
2 1/2 quarts uncoagulated blood
    6 hot red chile peppers, very finely
         chopped
    1 ounce (papeleta) dried ground clove
    1 ounce (papeleta) dried ground ani se
    3 ounces (papeletas) dried ground oregano
    3 ounces (papeletas) ground black pepper
    1 ounce (papeleta) ground cinnamon
      Salt to taste

Chop the onions and leeks very finely and cook slowly for about ten hours in lard or a little fat from the animal. As the mixture is heating, the onions and leeks will release the natural vegetable juices in which they will continue cooking. If the temperature is raised significantly, the abundant sugars in the onions can carmelize and even burn, something which should be avoided at all costs. After this cooking, the mixture should be like a thick puree of a creamy, brown color.

Chop the remaining fat very finely and place in a separate container. Mix in the blood, completely integrating the two ingredients. Then mix in the puree of onions and leeks. It is advantageous to combine these mixtures in a clay receptacle surrounded by lukewarm water. Otherwise the fat remains hardened and mixes badly.

Add the chopped peppers and spices and mix again to distribute uniformly. Stuff the mixture into cleaned intestines and stomach (or sausage casings) and scald until the mixture is well coagulated.

Prepare a broth with leeks and a little fresh fat and cook the sausages for 30 minutes at a slow boil. (With the broth left from the cooking of the sausages, it is the custome to prepare soup accompanied by slices of bread.)

Buzkantzak (also called odolkiak) can be simply boiled before being eaten. They can be baked or fried and are also excellent when cooked in cabbage or with beans.

Because these sausages are very fatty and strong tasting, they should not be eaten accompanied by water or weak wines.

BASQUE

BLOOD AND TONGUE SAUSAGES

- 16 fresh onions
- 4 ounces Prague powder No. 1
- 4 ounces black pepper
- 1 ounce ground marjoram
- 1 ounce thyme
- 1 ounce mace
- 32 ounces salt
- 36 pounds pork tongues
- 36 pounds pork snouts
- 14 pounds pork skins
- 14 pounds beef blood

Place pork tongues and snouts into a kettle and cook approximately 2 hours. Let it cool, then grind both through a 1 inch grinder plate. Grind pork skins through a 1/8 inch grinder plate. Dice pork fat into 1/4-3/4 inch cubes and scald for a few seconds using a sieve or screen.

Place all the meats and ingredients in a mixer and mix well. Stuff by hand into beef bungs and then place in a 195-200 degree F. water (but not boiling). Cook approximately 3 1/2 hours. Use a skewer to see if sausage is cooked sufficiently. Remove to container holding ice water, cooling enough so the sausage can be handled. Remove to 36-38 degrees F. cooler overnight. In the morning you will have 50 pounds of sausage. Surprise!

POLAND

> Poland: The Upier and Upiercsa were said to have slept in blood filled coffins.

WEST INDIAN PUMPKIN SAUSAGE

- 3 pounds sweet potatoes
- 2 pounds West Indian pumpkin (calabaza)
- 1 cup finely chopped shallots
- 1 tablespoon each thyme and marjoram
- 1 tablespoon fresh hot pepper, seeded and minced
- 1 teaspoon ground cloves
- Salt
- Pig's blood
- Pig's intestines

Have the intestines cleaned and ready. Peel and finely grate the sweet potatoes and pumpkin into a large bowl. Add the shallots, herbs, hot pepper and cloves. Season to taste with salt. Add enough pig's blood to give a fairly soft consistency. Fill the skins with the mixture, but do not pack tightly. Tie into lengths, or leave whole, tying at both ends with string.

Have ready a large pot of boiling salted water. As the sausages may burst if they rest on the bottom of the pot, place a trivet for the puddings to rest on. Poach them gently for about 20 minutes, or until no juice runs out when they are pricked.

About halfway through the cooking, the puddings will rise to the surface. Prick in 2 or 3 places with a large needle to expel air and prevent bursting. Drain and serve immediately, or cool and heat later. Serves 8 to 10 according to appetite.

BARBADOS

NOW THAT YOU'VE DROPPED IT!

OLD RODIKA'S HANDY HINT
FOR REMOVING BLOOD STAINS

Oh dear, what a mess! Well let old Rodika tell you what she always does. First, before using any detergents, old Rodika tries plenty of clear, cold water.

Then, if any stain remains, she cautiously tries applying a solution of ammonia and more cold water, but be sure to rinse quickly to avoid any discoloration.

APPENDIX A-

RECIPE VARIATIONS:
PUDDINGS AND MORE SAUSAGES

The preceding recipes have many variations which are valid to include, but may have such a slight difference, like a change in herb, that they do not seem to warrant an entire page devoted to them individually. Instead we decided to include them in the form of an appendix so the readers who are interested in the regional distinctions may have access to them.

The diversity of inclusions that follow may either serve as territorial information or may be taken as suggestions for individual taste and preference. The ensuing concepts follow a similar pattern as the book, as in breakfast, soup, pudding and sausage, but are separated by region.

SWEDEN

In Sweden, fried blood and Rye Meal Sausages are part of a traditional breakfast.

ENGLAND

In northern England sausages are often served at breakfast with fried apples or included in potato and mutton stews. In general, goose liver, rice, and raisins in goose skin casings are served in blood soup.

Favorite seasonings: coriander and caraway, in other parts marjoram and thyme.

DENMARK

Denmark has poached blood pudding, made with barley, apples, or ground pork. This is eaten either cold or fried in butter.

FLANDERS

Flanders is famous for a dried fruit-filled Boudin Noire grilled and served with applesauce.

FRANCE

The French are known for spinach and chestnuts in their puddings.

Favorite seasonings: in general, beetroot and garlic.

Languedoc: red pepper.

Alcase-Lorraine: apples.

Saint-Quentin in Picardy: onions.

NEDERLANDS

The Dutch have blood pudding with raisins.

PHILIPPINES

Another version of Dinuguan, also from the Philippines, uses coconut and lemon grass. The coconut meat and milk is scorched in a pan or on a grill (or on charcoal to be authentic) the water is then added and a thick cream is extracted. The rest of the recipe is about the same.

LOUISIANA CAJUN

In Cajun cooking, Boudin Noire is made with blood and rice and is called Boudin Rouge.

Favorite seasoning: sage.

BARBADOS

Blood puddings thickened with rice, sweet potato or bread and spiked with rum are considered essential for holiday celebration on Barbados. For pudding and souse, just thicken the blood sausages and headcheese.

CHILE

Chilean blood puddings are made from lamb and cooked in molds rather than casings.

CZECHOSLOVAKIA

The Czechs use blood and bread or barley and call the dish Jelita. They also use a blood sausage boiled in a pig's stomach and have named this Bachor.

GERMANY

Germans made blood sausages with large pieces of meat. Blutwurst is smoked and eaten cold, or poached and sliced, fried and served hot. Blut Zungenwurst is made with pork fat, blood and pickled tongue and is mosaic-like, while Speck Blutwurst reveals solid pieces of pork fat when sliced. Most are made with pig's blood.
Favorite seasonings: thyme and marjoram.

HUNGARY

In Hungary, the residents use bread and a small amount of ground pork and call the dish Veres Hurka.

KOREA

The only blood recipe the authors found containing noodles is a Korean dish called Soon Dai. With pork sausage, it contains rice noodles and giblets.

MEXICO

Mexico has a goat's blood sausage seasoned with fresh herbs and onions and stuffed into a goat's stomach.

SCOTLAND

In Scotland, black puddings are most likely made with sheep's blood and is usually just a white oatmeal pudding with blood added to it.

SLOVENIA

Blood sausage is a Slovenian country specialty, made along the same lines as the Polish recipe but thickened with millet and rice and flavored with dried mint, marjoram and sometimes paprika and garlic.

SPAIN

Morcillas are made in Spain, sometimes with rice. They can be poached or cooled and added to stews or sliced and fried. Also, morcillas can be wrapped in pastry. Fabada Asturiana is a bean soup including morcilla.

Favorite seasoning: fennel.

UKRAINE

There's a Ukrainian Christmas Blood Sausage with lingonberries.

Onion and Kasha Kishka may contain blood.

APPENDIX A+

HERBS AND SUCH

The pupose of this appendix is not to go indepth into every herb used in this book. It is assumed the readers will know most of them. Instead, this section is designed to touch on the terms the authors considered might be more obscure or archaic.

However, if any questions or further information is desired, the purchaser of this book is encouraged to write to the authors, in care of Mugwort Soup Publications. They will do their best to provide an informative and prompt response.

BOUQUET GARNI

This is just a few sprigs of thyme, a bay leaf, parsley and celery all tied together. This is used in many dishes and cooks who use them often tie several together and refrigerate for regular usage.

GARLIC

Allium Sativum Bewarum

Poor Man's Treacle, Clove Garlic

Alexander Neckam, a writer in the twelfth century, states this herb may be used as a pallialess In Virgel's 'Eclogues' we find this herb was largely consumed by the Greeks and Romans. However, we view this (dangerous) herb with the likes of Horace, as well as in the general outlook of Shakespear's time.

Horace detested garlic, calling it "more Poisoness than hemlock", and tells of how he was made ill at the table of Maecenas. Those of Shakespear's time merely conserned the smell of it as a sign of vulgarity.

The ancient Greeks did not allow those who partook of garlic to enter the temple of Cybele, whose highlight of worship included the 'Taurobolium'. This was the baptism in the blood of the Sacred Bull, signifying her dying-God Consort. If for private reasons you, the reader, avoid this herb, rest assured you dwell in good company.

MUNCHKIN

This is a Scottish term, meaning pint.

ROUX

1/2 cup oil
1/2 cup all-purpose flour

Heat the oil in a heavy skillet over a medium flame, then add the flour, stirring constantly. Continue to stir until roux turns lightly brown.

Lower the heat and continue stirring until roux reaches the desired degree of doneness. Can take from 1/2 hour to 1 hour to finish. It can be kept indefinitely in storage, and if it separates simply stir back together.

The successful way of making a good roux is to sprinkle flour slowly into the shortening. Then add cold water to the stock, as hot water bleaches the roux.

TANSY

Tanacetum Vulgare

Bitter Buttons, Hinheal, Parsley Fern

Tansy is not included in the recipes in this book, although it was originally in some of the recipes we found. We did not include it because its general use today is as an insect repellant and the medicinal use for tansy is to expel worms. Instead we inserted appropriate substitutes of either thyme or sage, depending on the overall flavor of the fare.

TOCINO

This is simply salted pork fat.

VET-SIN

Monosodium Glutamate

This can cause headaches in some people.

APPENDIX B-

Direct from the Carpathian Mountains

This and the next appendix contain the recipes the authors found in the midnight hours under the light of the full moon in obscure libraries. For reasons which will become clear, they could not resist slipping them into this book, although strickly speaking, these are dishes which do not contain blood.

SZÉKELY GULYAS

Transylvanian Goulash

While not strictly a blood recipe it does seem to be within the theme and besides, who knows when normals may drop by? (Plus you can always add a blood sauce for **some** portions)

- 1 pound sauerkraut
- 2 tablespoons lard
- 1 cup finely chopped onions
- 1/4 teaspoon finely chopped garlic
- 2 tablespoons sweet Hungarian paprika
- 3 cups chicken stock or water
- 2 pounds boneless shoulder of pork, cut into 1" cubes
- 1 1/2 teaspoons caraway seeds
- 1/4 cup tomato puree
- Salt
- 1/2 cup sour cream
- 1/2 cup heavy cream
- 2 tablespoons flour

Wash sauerkraut thoroughly under cold running water, then soak in cold water for 10-20 minutes to reduce its sourness.

Melt the lard in a five quart casserole and add the onions. Cook them over a moderate heat, stirring occasionally, for 6-8 minutes, or until they are lightly colored, then add the garlic and cook 1-2 minutes longer. Off the heat, stir in the paprika, continuing to stir until the onions are well coated. Pour in 1/2 cup stock or water and bring it to a boil, then add the pork cubes.

Now spread the sauerkraut over the pork and sprinkle it with the caraway seeds. In a small bowl, combine the tomato puree and the rest of the stock or water, and pour the mixture over the sauerkraut. Bring the liquid to a boil once more, then reduce the heat to its' lowest point, cover the casserole tightly and let simmer for 1 hour. Check every now and then to be sure the liquid has not cooked away. Add a little stock or water if it has; the sauerkraut should stay moist.

When the pork is tender, combine the sour cream and heavy cream in a mixing bowl. Beat the flour into the cream with a wire whisk, then carefully stir this mixture into the casserole. Simmer for 10 minutes longer. Taste for seasoning. Serve Transylvanian goulash in deep individual plates, accompanied by a bowl of sour cream.

Serves 4-6

CARPATHIA

APPENDIX B+

BAT GOD OF THE VALLEY OF OAXACA

A recent find in Chalco, a city on the southern edge of Mexico City, Mexico, was a ceramic figure of a bat god. This is an anthropomorphised figure with the claws and facial features of a bat.

In the Valley of Oaxaca, in about 100-800 AD, the culture of the Zapotecs flourished. So far, the bat god is most closely associated with those people.

SAUTÉED BATS

According to a professor in Martinique, there are three species of fruit-eating bats in the West Indies that are good eating.

- 2 bats
- 2 tablespoons butter
- 8 slices bacon
- 4 scallions
- 2 cloves garlic
- 1 glass rum
- 1 bouquet garni
- 1 glass red wine
- Salt & pepper to taste
- 1 tablespoon flour
- Croutons

Remove the heads, wings and feet. Skin, and remove viscera. Rinse out and lightly salt. Rinse and dry. Sauté the bats in the butter, and cut the bacon into small pieces and add together with the scallions and garlic. When the bats are lightly browned, heat the rum and pour over them. Ignite and let the flame die out. Add the red wine and the bouquet garni. Simmer for thirty minutes, then thicken with flour mixed with a little water. Serve with hot buttered croutons.

WEST INDIES

KO E ME'AKAI FAKA-TONGA

Tonga Fruit Bat

      Fruit bats (1 per person)
1   quart coconut cream

Singe bats in a fire and remove skin. Split open the chest and remove intestines.

Marinate bats in coconut cream. This will make them more tender and aromatic. Place in ground oven, checking frequently. Remove when meat falls away from the bones.

Alternately, after singeing and cleaning, place chest down on hot coals and cook, turn when side is cooked.

May be eaten immediately.

TONGA

PE'A

Baked Bat

Bats (1 per person)
Salt, pepper
Onions

Skin or flame bats to remove hair. Eviscerate and cut into small pieces. Bake in a ground oven or "umu" over hot rocks.

Alternately, season with salt and pepper and stir fry with onions.

SAMOA

APPENDIX O

PLANNING A COMPLETE MEAL

Here is a fun and entertaining plan for a complete meal, especially designed for your next gloaming garden party. As your crepuscular friends and fiends visit, the following may be presented.

For the hors d'oeuvres try the CANAPES from Chapter Two. The MUSHROOM DUXELLES have just the right flavor to whet the appetite. An optional salad may be in order next. But nothing heavier than a small green salad, served with a vinigrette dressing.

Then a nice POTAGE D'ALOSE from Chapter Four is perfect for the first serving. Shad, a nice fish, will be a pleasing prelude for the main course.

For the main course we suggest the PATAGONIAN MIXTA. This is in Chapter Five and contains a variety of meats. An excellant sampler, it is grilled, and with some practice can be entertaining to watch being prepared. Much of the slicing can be done ahead of time, allowing you to give an enjoyable presentation. It is also served with a delectable SPICEY DIPPING SAUSE. This can be prepared the night before, chilled, and then allowed to reach room temperature (perfect for serving) on your patio while you prepare the meal.

As an after dinner treat, blood oranges, lingonberries, and gouda cheese would be perfect. The gouda cheese is mild, and is smoothly pleasant to the tongue in sharp contrast to the sweet-tart tastes of the fruit. As an alternative, pomegranates may be served. If so, it may add to the presentation to slice them in half for your guests. Then scoop out the pulp while squeezing the rind, causing it to 'bleed' over itself with a flair.

With the dinner serve Egri Bikaver (Bulls Blood) wine at room temperature. This completes one variation of a truly social dinner occasion. Done with style this can be a charming feast for the whole clan.

BIBLIOGRAPHY

VAMPIRE LORE

Barber, Paul. Vampires, Burial & Death. New Haven: Yale University Press, 1988.

Cammarota, M. D. Jr. I Vampiri. Rome: Fanucci Editore, 1984.

Copper, Basil. The Vampire in Legend, Fact and Art. London: Corgi Books, 1975.

Dumas, Francois Ribadeau. À La Recherche des Vampires. Verviers, Belgium: Bibliotheque Marabout, 1976.

Farson, Daniel. The Beaver Book of Horror. London: Beaver Books, 1977.

Garden, Nancy. Vampires. New York: Bantam Books, 1973.

Hill, Douglas. The History of Ghosts, Vampires & Werewolves. Baltimore: Harrow Books, 1973.

Hurwood, Bernhardt J. Monsters and Nightmares. New York: Belmont Books, 1967.

────── Monsters Galore. Greenwich, Connecticut: Gold Medal Books, 1965.

────── The Monstrous Undead. New York: Lancer Books, 1963.

―――― Passport to Horror. New York: New American Library, 1973.

―――― Vampires, Werewolves & Ghouls. New York: Ace Books, 1968.

―――― Vampires, Werewolves & Other Demons. New York: Scholastic Book Services, 1972.

J.S.D., "Return of the Bat God". Archaeology. September, 1992, pg. 46.

Jones, Ernest. On the Nightmare. New York: Liveright, 1951.

Masters, Anthony. The Natural History of the Vampire. New York: Berkley Medallion Books, 1972.

Masters, R. E. L. Eros and Evil. New York: Matrix House, 1966.

McNally, Raymond. Dracula Was a Woman. New York: McGraw-Hill, 1983.

McNally, Raymond T. & Florescu, Radu. In Search of Dracula. New York: Warner Paperback Library, 1973.

Perkowski, Jan L. The Darkling, A Treatise on Slavic Vampirism. Columbus, Ohio: Slavica Publishers, 1989.

Ronan, Margaret & Eve. Curse of the Vampires. New York: Scholastic Books, 1979.

Ronay, Gabriel. The Truth About Dracula. New York: Stein and Day, 1974.

Sturm, Dieter & Voelker, Klaus. Von denen Vampiren oder Menschensaugern. Munich: Carl Hanser Verlag, 1968.

Summers, Montague. The Vampire His Kith and Kin. New York: E. P. Dutton, 1929.

────── The Vampire in Europe. New York: University Books, 1961.

Vallejo, Boris. 'Boris Vallejo's 1993 Mythology Calendar'. New York: Workman Publishing Company, 1992

Villeneuve, Roland. Loups-Garous et Vampires. Paris: J'ai Lu, 1970.

Volta, Ornella. The Vampire. London: Tandem Books, 1965.

Walker, Barbara G. The Woman's Encyclopedia of Myths and Secrets. New York: HarperSanFrancisco, a division of HarperCollins Publishers, 1983.

Wright, Dudley. The Book of Vampires. New York: Causeway Books, 1973.

BIBLIOGRAPHY

COOKBOOKS

Aidells, Bruce and Kelly, Denis. <u>Hot Links and Country Flavors</u>. Alfred A Knopf, New York, 1990.

Chantraine, Charles. <u>La Cuisine Chantraine</u>. Barrows and Company, New York, 1966.

Crocker, Betty. <u>Betty Crocker's Cookbook</u>. Golden Press, New York. 1986.

Dayrit, Patt Limjuco. <u>Favorite Filipino Recipes</u>. Books for Pleasure, Philippines, 1975.

Dorje, Rinjing. <u>Food in Tibetan Life</u>. Prospect Books, London, 1985.

Elbert, Virginia and George A. <u>Down-Island Caribbean Cookery</u>. Simon and Schuster, New York, 1991.

Elkon, Juliette. <u>A Belgian Cookbook</u>. Cudahy, New York, 1958.

Elleson, S. Audrey. <u>Great Scandinavian Cookbook</u>. Crown, New York, 1967.

Fitzgibbon, Theodora. <u>A Taste of Ireland</u>. Haughton Mufflin, Boston, 1969.

Frederick, Justice George. <u>Pennsylvania Dutch Cookery</u>. The Business Bourse, New York, 1935.

Grieve, Mrs. M. <u>A Modern Herbal Vol. I</u>. Dover Publications, New York, 1971.

Grigson, Jane. <u>The Art Making sausages, Pates, and other of Charcuterie</u>. Alfred A Knopf, New York, 1966.

Guermont, Claude and Paul Frmkin. The Norman Table. Charles Scribners Sons, New York, 1958.

Kakonen, Ulla. Natural Cooking the Finnish Way. Quadrangle, New York, 1974.

Kennedy, Diana. The Art of Mexican Cooking. Bantam, New York, 1989.

Kovis, Paul. Transylvanian Cuisine. Crown, New York, 1985.

Lambert, Elizabeth. The Complete Book of Caribbean Cooking. New York, 1967.

Lang, George. The Cuisine of Hungary. Athenaeum, New York, 1985.

Latimer, Norma and Gordon. Olde English Traditional Country Style Recipes. Compiled and printed by the authors in Culver City, 1984.
Mabey, Richard. The New Age Herbalist. Collier Books, New York. 1988.

Merinoff, Linda. The Savory Sausage. Poseidon, New York, 1986.

No Author. Cajun Cuisine. Beau Bayou Publishing Company, United States. 1985.

No Author. Polish Cookbook. Culinary Arts Institute, Melrose Park, 1976.

No Author. The Cooking of Vienna's Empire. Time Life Books, Foods of the World. 1968.

No Author. The Gourmet Cookbook Volume I. Gourmet Distributing Company, New York, 1950.

Pula, Tupou L. Tongan Food. University of Alaska, Anchorage, 1980.

Ranhoter, Charles. *The Epicurean*. Dover, New York, 1971.

Rose, Peter G. *The Sensible Cook: Dutch Foodways in the Old and New World*. Syracuse University, New York, 1989.

Scharfenberg, Horst. *The Cuisines of Germany*. Poseidon, New York, 1980.

Schulman, Estella Francesca. *Now Listen Good*. North River, 1979.

Schwabe, Calvin W. *Unmentionable Cuisine*. University Press of Virginia, Charlottesville, 1979.

Souli, Sophia. *The Greek Cookery Book*. Michalis Toumbas Publications S.A., Athens, 1989.

Tannanhill, Reay. *Food in History*. Stein and Day, New York, 1987.

Wise, Naomi. *Meat and Game Cooking*. Chevron Chemical Company, San Ramon, 1988.

INDEX

A

Adam 92
Africa 29, 93
Animal wombs 94
Apicius 94
Arabs 25
Arctic 34
Argentina 76
Armenia 93, 100
Asanbosam 29
Ashantiland 29
Austria 54, 55

B

Babylon
Bachor 117
Baked Bat 130
Banana leaves 77
Barbados 113, 117
Basque 18, 94, 111
Bat God of the Valley of Oaxaca 127
Bathory, Countess Elzebet 82
Beef Covered with Blood 70
Belgium 38, 93, 103
  Flanders 116
Berbers 25
Black Breakfast 19
Black Pudding 89
Black Pudding in County Cork 81

Black Sausage 100, 101, 102, 104
Black Sausages 110
Blodpølse
Blood
  Anti-coagulants 13-14
  Blood Heat 26
  Blood per volume 65
  Coagulation temperature 45
  How to remove 114
  How to taste 9
  Lean times 14
  Nutritional information 14
  Where to buy 13
Blood and Milk 12, 25
Blood and Tongue Sausage 112
Blood Breakfast Cakes 22
Blood from a Scot's Kitchen 85
Blood Loaf 69
Blood Pancakes 17
Blood Pudding Sausage 106
Blood Sausage 95
Blood Sausage in Green Sauce 72
Blood Sausage Tacos 71
Blood Sausages, origins 93
Blut Zugenwurst 118
Blutgasse 82
Blutwurst / Applesauce & Mashed Potatoes 42
Boudin d'Auvergne 102
Boudin de Lapin 109
Boudin de Noel 103
Boudin Noir 23, 116, 117
Boudin Noir au Cerfeuil 106
Boudin Rouge 117
Brittany 102

Bruchfleisch 54
Bruculaco 36
Bull's Blood 26, 132
Buzkantzak 110, 111

C

Cajun Boudin Rouge 96
Calf Lung Stew 64
Camel Hair and Blood 25
Canapés 32, 132
Cardinal Humours 25
Carpathian Mountains 82
Carribean 69
Chile 117
Ch'Ling Shih 63
China 62, 63
Chinese Chicken Blood Soup 62
Christmas Sausage 103, 119
Ciuatete 71
Civet de Lièvre 48
Civet de Mou de Veau 64
Cocido Madrileno o Olla Podrido 52
Cooked Green Tomato Sauce 72
Corn husks 77
Crostini 31
Crusades 93
Czarnina 46
Czechoslovakia 117

D

de Arc, Joan 28
de Rais, Gille 28
Dearg-Dul 81

Denmark 116
Dinuguan 57, 117
Disclaimers 9
Dixmude 38
Dogs 65, 66
Dracula (Vlad Tepes) 13, 24, 82
Drenthe 39
Drisheen 12, 81
Duck Soup 46

E

Eger Region 26
Egri Bikaver 26, 132
England 13, 50, 79, 90, 91, 116
English Black Pudding 90
English Fairy tale 91
Epic of Gilgamesh 92
Ethyl alcohol 34
Eyrbyggia 34

F
Faeada Asturiana 119
Farkaskoldus 70
Filets de Lièvre à la Provençale 68
Filipines 13
Finland 17, 61, 93
France
  Alsace-Lorraine 116
  Auvergne 102
  Bordeux 94
  Languedoc 116
  Normandy 107
  Provence 68
  Saint-Quentin 116

French Boudin 89
French Delicacy 12
French Style Chicken in Blood Sauce 78
Frikatza 18

G

Gaetano Mammore 30
Germany 43, 55, 118
  Rhineland 42
Ghana 51
Gilgamesh 92
Glass of Blood 13
Goose Blood Pudding 87
Greece 36, 37
Groats-Gut Beuling 44
Guinea 29
Gyuma 66, 95

H

Hare Fillets Province Style 68
Hare Soup 50
Hawaii 65
Heaven and Earth 40
Herrerosland 29
Hete Bliksem 39
Himmel on Ard met Blootwoosch 42
Himmel und Erde 40
Honourable Mother 71
Hot Bloodmeat Cereal 21
Hot Lightning 39
Hungary 26, 70, 74, 118
Hutyu 100

I

Iceland 34
Indonesia
  Celebes 20
  Sulawesi 20
Ireland 12, 81
  Cork Market 81
  Derry 14
  Tipperary 81
  Tyrone 14
Italy 30, 31, 93, 104

J

Jelita 117
Jugged Hare 48

K

Kasha Kishka 119
Kishka 105
Kiskil-lilla 92
Kiszka z Krwia 108
Ko E Me'Akai Faka-Tonga 129
Korea 118

L

Lamb's Blood Pudding 86
Lamia 104
Lampreys 67
Lamproie à la Bordalaise 67
Lebanon 93
Les Toastes Sanguinares 38

Lilith 92
Lilitu 92
Liver Pate 31
Loango 29
Lord of the Mictlampa 71

M

Madrid Stew 52
Mahr 82
Marco Polo 26
Masai 26
Meat Stew 51
Mexican Blood Sausage 98
Mexico 71, 73, 99, 118
Mice in Cream 34
Mictecaciuatl: Lady of the Place of Death 71
Milo 36
Mixed Organ Stew 54
Mjertovjec 105
Mongols 26
Moribondo 102
Moronga en Salsa Verde 72
Moronga Mexiquense 98
Mushroom Duxelles 32, 132
Myma 37

N

Nadorispan 70
Nederlands 39, 44, 59, 117
Nice French Stew 58
Norway 21
Ntsin 51
Nuer Roasts 29

O

Odolkiak 111
Otgiruru 29
Owenga 29
Owl 92
Ox 85

P

Palatine-Viceroy 1826 Cooking Volume 70
Patagonian Mixed Grill 75
Patagonian Parillada Mixta 75, 132
Patzinak tribes 26
Pe'a 130
Pennsylvania Dutch Black Soup 59
Philipines 57, 117
Phoenicia 93
Pig Organ Sausages 108
Poland 46, 93, 108, 112
Portugal 93
Potage d'Alose 56, 130
Poulet au Sang 78
Princess Palatine of Louis XIV 84
Pudding Cakes 20

Q

Quick Meat Consummé 58

R

Rabbit Sausages 109
Roasted Pig Organs 77

Romania 93
  Carpathia 126
  Transylvania 93
  Wallachia 24
Rotton Pot 52
Russia 93, 105
Rye Meal Sausages 116

S

Salsa de Tomate Verde Cocida 72
Salsiccia d'Italia 104
Samoa 65, 77, 130
Sardinia 30
Saucisse en Croute 27
Sautéed Bats 128
Sawney Bean 85
Scotland 22, 85, 86, 87, 118
  Edinburgh 85
Scrambled Blood and Eggs 18
Sea Yrchins 79
Shad Broth 56, 132
Shwarz Sauer 59
Slovenia 118
Snagov 24
Soon Dai 118
Soul cakes 38, 55
Spain 53, 119
Speck Blutwurst 118
Spicey Blood Sausage 96
Spicey Dipping Sause 76, 132
Spicy Cajun Style Blood Pudding 88
Steer 65
Stoker, Bram 13, 24
Stuffed Pig's Stomach 74

Sumer 92
Summers, Montague 55
Svartsoppa 60
Sweden 61, 116
Swedish Black Soup 60
Switzerland 41
Székely Gulyás 125

T

Tacos de Moronga 71
Tanzania 26
Terrapin 80
Ti Sheh Tan 62
Tibet 66, 95
Timpanita 36
Tofu 62
Toltott Malac Gyomr 74
Tonga 77, 129
Tonga Fruit Bat 129
Totoga 77
Transylvanian Goulash 125
Turks 24
Turtle 80
Tyre 93

U

Ukraine 119
Upier 46, 112
Upiercsa 46, 112
Upierczi 105
USA
  Alaska 34
  Louisiana Cajun 88, 97, 117

Ozarks 80
Pennsylvania Dutch 59
Rocky Mountains 97
Slave Coast 97

V

Vampire in a Coffin 27
Vampiro 53
Veres Hurka 118
Veriletet 17
Victorian Era 13
Vienna 82
Vietnam 13, 20
Vlad the Impaler 24

W

Wallachia 24
West Indian Pumpkin Sausages 113
West Indies 128
White sauce 34
Wieszczy 46
Wume 97

Y

Yrchins 79
Yugoslavia
  Croatia 93
  Slovenia 93

Z

Zapotecs 127

About the Authors

Ardin C. Price, a writer and educator, is an ordained clergyman. He has been actively involved in the field of preternatural creatures for over twenty years.

Trishna Leszczyc comes from an ancient Polish family who's history has intertwined with Vampire lore for centuries. A researcher who has done investigative writing, she is currently working on her first novel.

OTHER RECIPES AND NOTES

OTHER RECIPES AND NOTES

OTHER RECIPES AND NOTES

Send us your favorite blood recipe!

Name_____

City:_____State:_____Zip:_____

If your recipe is used in the revised edition you will receive acknowledgement in print and a free copy of the book. All submissions must comform to copyright laws. No other form of payment is promised or implied. Please sign below that you understand these conditions.

Signature_____

Special Order Form

Telephone Information: Call: (205) 837-7628 or Fax: (310) 478-7124

Postal Orders: Mugwort Soup Publications, PO Box 11183, Huntsville, Al, 35814-1183. USA. (205) 837-7628

Please send the following books. I understand that I may return any books for a full refund - for any reason, no questions asked.

Company Name:

_____
Name:

_____

City: _____

State: _____ Zip: _____-_____

Number of copies _____ x $14.95

Sales tax (Alabama) add 8%   _____
Shipping: $2.05 first book only:
    More than 1 FREE
                                  Total _____

Check or Money Order only please

Name of person you would like on our mailing list:

Name_____

City:_____ State____ Zip_____

Special Order Form

Telephone Information: Call: (205) 837-7628 or Fax: (310) 478-7124

Postal Orders: Mugwort Soup Publications, PO Box 11183, Huntsville, Al, 35814-1183. USA. (205) 837-7628

Please send the following books. I understand that I may return any books for a full refund - for any reason, no questions asked.

Company Name:

_____
Name:

_____

City: _____

State: _____ Zip: _____-_____

Number of copies _____ x $14.95

Sales tax (Alabama) add 8%   _____
Shipping: $2.05 first book only:
    More than 1 FREE   _____
                                Total   _____

Check or Money Order only please

Name of person you would like on our mailing list:

Name_____

City:_____State:_____Zip:_____